This book is to be returned on or before
the last date stamped below.

01. AUG	7 JUN 1997	27 FEB 2003
17. FEB 96	-6 JAN 1998	28 JUN 2003
23 OCT	03 NOV 1998	J
7 JAN 97	-2 JUL 1999	- 1 MAY 2007
15 APR 1997	28 APR 2001	17 OCT 2007
	15 May 2001	
06 MAY 1997	20 OCT 2001 RH	
06 MAY 1997	- 3 APR 2002	
	24 JAN 2003	

SUTTON LEISURE SERVICES

RENEWALS Please quote: date of return, your ticket number
and computer label number for each item.

REMBRANDT

REMBRANDT

Emmanuel Starcky

STUDIO EDITIONS

LONDON

First published by Fernand Hazan, Paris in 1990

First published in Great Britain in 1990 by Studio Editions Ltd
Translation by John Greaves

This revised edition published in 1993 by Studio Editions Ltd
Princess House, 50 Eastcastle Street
London W1N 7AP

Copyright © 1993 Studio Editions Ltd

ISBN 1 85170 902 9

Printed and bound in Hong Kong

Frontispiece: Self-Portrait Holding his Palette, Brushes and Maulstick,
c.1663. The Trustees of the Iveagh Bequest, Kenwood, London

INTRODUCTION

Rembrandt spent his life pursuing the expression of values in which he passionately believed. He has been popularly misconceived as an enigma. This is basically false in that the only perceivable enigma is the one Rembrandt himself recognized: how to ask questions to which there are no answers; how to go on putting the questions in a different way in the full recognition of the limitations of human understanding. His passion was a passion for honesty in terms of himself and integrity in terms of his art.

Possessing both good and bad qualities, Rembrandt had the strength to accept this and the desire to overcome his weaknesses. It is probably true, for example, that after the death of his wife Saskia, he rejected a woman whom he had promised to marry. His companion for a while, she did not respond well to his denials and threatened to bring him down with her accusations. Whatever the details of this episode, suffice it to say that Rembrandt was prepared to pay the price of his unethical behaviour in order to keep his extraordinary creative powers intact. It was these powers which enabled him to survive the cruellest changes of fortune in his family life and to weather the storms of bereavement and bankruptcy.

Rembrandt wanted to give his all. The concept of genius, which is closely linked to the concept of a creative force, suggests some kind of transcendent reality, placing the artist on a higher plane, above other people, where his work does not need to be understood. In this book, we have tried to avoid demonstrating Rembrandt's genius, but have sought instead to situate the artist in the context of his times, in order to illuminate his life and his work and, finally, to reach a better understanding of the universal nature of his art.

Seventeenth-century artists in France and Italy often depicted a world peopled by heroes or gods. The same tendency prevailed in the Low Countries and for a certain time manifested itself in Rembrandt's work. But collectors and lovers of art, of whom there were many in his homeland, were hungry for simpler images that corresponded more closely to daily life. Dutch artists were therefore freed from the obligation to create a world of the ideal. In this sense, while remaining one of the most fascinating artists of the seventeenth century, Rembrandt was not an innovator, strictly speaking. His work is not the expression of an artist seeking to confirm his identity as the creator of a new and different world.

Initially, he wished to reach the top rung of a social ladder upon which his contemporaries conferred a great deal of importance. Clearly, he needed to gain a certain security in order to achieve a sense of personal freedom. But little by little he was able to abandon this preoccupation. Looking at a Rembrandt painting, we feel no need to observe a respectful distance; rather, we move closer, to understand it better; we are involved. Rembrandt had no desire to set up any ideal of beauty of the kind found in contemporary Italian painting, for example. He used his prodigious talent to further a vision which was to grow more profound as the years went by.

His religious scenes soon began to distinguish themselves from the traditional formulae of his contemporaries, taking the form of a testament to a personal spiritual quest. Here we are presented with a startling paradox: that one of the greatest religious painters of all time lived in a country, the Netherlands, governed by a Protestant oligarchy. However, the paradox is merely superficial: while the religious image was discouraged in places of Protestant worship, a degree of tolerance and sincere piety, as was practised by diverse faiths, gave conscientious licence to this kind of representation.

It has been generally agreed that Rembrandt was an exception, an anomaly in the context of Dutch art which, for the most part, restricted itself to realist representation. He was the exception that proved the rule. Paul Claudel summed up Rembrandt's role by describing his achievement as 'a triumphant fathoming of the depths'.

When Rembrandt was born, the Dutch were on the verge of gaining their independence. A certain number of factors contributed to the remarkable artistic proliferation in the Low Countries at the beginning of the seventeenth century.

In recent political history, a series of dramatic events had engendered a spirit of determination. The sixteenth century was a period of Spanish domination, increasingly resented by the indigenous population, which expressed its fury in the insurrection of 1568. This gave rise to a fierce and bloody repression wrought by the Duke of Alba. However, Dutch resistance finally brought about a partition between the Northern and Southern States in 1579. The Union of Arras reinforced the links between the Catholic States of the South and the King of Spain, whereas the Union of Utrecht began a process of unification among the Northern Dutch States which, in 1588, became the Republic of United Provinces. A truce with Spain was not concluded until 1609. The will to shake off the yoke of tyranny, to be free of oppression

and fear, brought victory over the Spanish troops. Though Spain was one of the greatest European powers at the time, not even its vastly superior forces could prevent the Dutch from gaining a glorious victory. The rise of the merchant class, which was an integral factor in the development of towns, creating an urban network unparalleled in the whole of Europe, finally gave birth to the Republic. The violent and committed reaction to despotism found its immediate corollary in the confirmation of a political identity and an acute appreciation of liberty.

The fierce struggle for independence had a profound effect on the Dutch mentality. The Dutch had learned how to turn adversity to their advantage. It is tempting to view the intense artistic activity at the beginning of the seventeenth century as an indirect reflection of recent historical events. For religious and political reasons, this new-found liberty fostered in the minds of many an aversion to intolerance. The seven provinces of this little republic now sent their representatives to a States General. The nobility, decimated by the struggle against Spain, found itself losing its grip on power, which now remained – in peacetime – in the hands of a cultivated bourgeois oligarchy. At the head of the administrative hierarchy were the senior civil servants, the pensionaries. The Grand Pensionary was the representative of the province of Holland, the richest of the seven. Originally, the Stadtholder had been the representative of the king or the emperor in each province. Stadtholder William the Silent, who had led the insurrection, could no longer represent the Spanish sovereign; in fact, he was assassinated by the Spanish in 1584. From now on the Stadtholder took his authority from the provincial States, intervening in the event of a military threat and, in such a case, assuming the role of admiral-in-chief. However, both the States General and the Grand Pensionary played a determining political role in the life of the country. There were inevitable and frequent disagreements between these two branches of the executive power. Such differences had their repercussions – or their outlet – in religious

Map showing the seventeen provinces of the Netherlands,
by Nicholas Visscher, c.1680.
Royal Geographical Society, London

quarrels of sometimes dramatic proportions. Nonetheless, on the whole, the tranquillity of life in the Dutch Republic at that time was renowned. Descartes, who lived in Holland from 1629 to 1649 (and was painted by Frans Hals), recognized this in a letter to Guez de Balzac written in 1631: 'Is there any other country in the world where one could be more free, where one could sleep in greater tranquillity, where one would have less to fear, where the law is a better protection against crime, where poisoning, treason and calumnies would be less commonplace, where there remain more traces of the happy and tranquil innocence of our forefathers?'

It was in this atmosphere, conducive to creativity, that Rembrandt spent his youth. The two towns in which he lived, Leiden and Amsterdam, were in the province of Holland, the name used out of convenience to designate the whole country. Situated between the Zuiderzee and the mouth of the Rhine, this was the richest, most influential and dynamic province in the country. Furthermore, it contained two fifths of the young republic's population.

Rembrandt's family came from Leiden. The city had been besieged twice by the Spanish (1573–4) and its heroic resistance was rewarded by the foundation of a university in 1575. In 1606, the year of the artist's birth, the inhabitants of Leiden numbered about 17,000. Textile production played a large part in the life of the town, but Leiden was also known as one of the principal intellectual and artistic centres in the country. The internationally renowned sculptor Hendrick de Keyser and the still life painter Jan Davidsz. de Heem, who was an exact contemporary of Rembrandt, both worked there at various times. The most famous portrait painters in the town were J. van Ravesteyn and Joris van Schooten. Particular mention should be made of the landscape artist Jan van Goyen, a native of Leiden, who is recorded as being there between 1627 and 1632. We should also draw attention to the 'pre-Rembrandtist' painter Jacob Pynas, who contributed to Rembrandt's development and seems to have spent some time in Leiden around 1626.

Not far from Leiden, between Amsterdam and the sea, stood the city of Haarlem. The young Rembrandt could scarcely have been unaware of the intense artistic activity there, only twenty miles or so from his home town. Haarlem had been besieged by the Spanish in 1572–3, and had been forced to surrender. It was some years before the town recovered its dynamism. The closing of the port of Antwerp in 1585 had a decisive economic effect on the northern provinces, however, and among the many emigrating Flemish and Walloons a large number settled in Haarlem.

With the foundation of an academy in 1587, Karel van Mander, Hendrick Goltzius and Cornelis van Haarlem gave a fresh impetus to this artistic centre. They inspired a belated Mannerist movement of considerable importance. In 1622 there were more than 40,000 inhabitants in the town. Among them were the great portrait painter Frans Hals and the celebrated landscape artists Esaias van de Velde, Hercules Seghers and Salomon van Ruysdael. We can be sure that such painters made an impression on Rembrandt; he is known to have reworked a Seghers etching and he owned eight of his paintings.

Utrecht, which gave its name to another province, was a little further away from Leiden, but its privileged relationship with Rome and Italy – Utrecht was to remain the seat of future papal representatives – explains its attraction for many Catholic painters. The young Rembrandt was greatly influenced by the painters of Utrecht. The engraver H. Goudt returned from Italy in 1611. He diffused throughout the United Provinces an intimate knowledge of the works of the German artist Adam Elsheimer. A generation of artists led by Abraham Bloemaert, and including Hendrick Terbrugghen and Gerard van Honthorst, returned from Italy between 1615 and 1620. Having responded directly to the teaching of Caravaggio, they proved, in turn, a more or less direct influence on Rembrandt. There is no actual evidence that the master went to Utrecht, but the town is situated on the road to Friesland, which Rembrandt took in 1634 on his way to marry Saskia.

Amsterdam, which had become in many respects the most important centre in the country, was built on a vast number of little islands on the banks of two rivers, the Ijssel and the Amstel. In 1622 there were about 105,000 inhabitants in the city. As in Haarlem, the demographic growth can be explained by the high level of immigration fostered by religious tolerance. Economically the town was enjoying a period of expansion while the rest of Europe was in recession. The decline of Antwerp as a maritime and commercial centre and the geographical proximity of Amsterdam to northern Europe stimulated this development. The important network of maritime trade which the Hollanders and Zeelanders had established with the rest of the world had its centre in Amsterdam. By the end of the sixteenth century, the Dutch fleet had grown considerably and was to dominate the seas until at least 1670. It is estimated that Dutch naval strength accounted for three-quarters of European shipping. The famous East India Company was founded in 1602, whilst the Bank of Amsterdam was created in 1609; the first European stock-exchange was established in Amsterdam. Most of the population was employed by the textile industry and the shipyards, or in other manufacturing businesses. The intellectual life of the city centred on such names as the physician Christian Huygens, the microbiologist Anthon van Leeuwenhoek and the philosopher Baruch Spinoza. The *Illustrius Athenaeum*, the great Amsterdam school, was inaugurated in 1632. Musical life was represented by the composer and organist of the Oude Kerk, Jan Sweelinck (1562–1621), whose pupils included J. Schulz, better known as Praetorius. Finally, in the realm of the fine arts, we should note the activity of a small group of young artists, most of them Catholics, who originated a renaissance in history painting, and were later to be known as the 'pre-Rembrandtists'. Most of them had travelled to Italy where they were influenced by Elsheimer and Caravaggio. The most important names in this group of painters were Pieter Lastman, Jan and Jacob Pynas and Claes Moeyaert.

Rembrandt's father was a prosperous miller in Leiden. His mill was on a tributary of the 'Old Rhine' or 'Oude Rijn': hence the addition of van Rijn to his name, which became Harmen Gerritszoon van Rijn. A convert to Calvinism, he married Neeltgen Willemsdochter Zuytbrouck, a young Catholic girl, in October 1589; the union was to produce at least ten children. The ninth, Rembrandt Harmenszoon van Rijn, was born in Leiden on 15 July 1606. At the age of eleven he was sent to the Latin School. According

to Orlers, mayor and chronicler of Leiden, Rembrandt's parents took him out of this school so that he might learn the art of painting. What we know for sure is that Rembrandt, at the age of thirteen, enrolled at the university in Leiden, his home town. It is quite probable that his parents took this decision, weighing the economic advantages of such scholarship against the possibilities available to a budding artist. As it turned out, Rembrandt never studied there for any length of time.

Rembrandt began his training as an artist under the tutelage of Jacob I. van Swanenburgh, a history painter who had spent some time in Naples and had recently returned home to Leiden. Around 1624, Rembrandt moved to Amsterdam where he worked in the studio of Pieter Lastman (1583–1633). Lastman, a Catholic, had also been in Italy, returning to Holland around 1607. His compositional style had considerable influence on the young Rembrandt as, one suspects, did the work of Jacob Pynas, whose studio Rembrandt frequently visited.

Returning to Leiden in 1625, Rembrandt set up his own independent studio. The first work whose date can be authenticated is *The Stoning of St Stephen* of 1625 (page 45), followed by *The Angel and the Prophet Balaam* (see page 11) and *The Baptism of the Eunuch* (Utrecht, Rijksmuseum, 'Het Catharijnconvent'), all dated 1626, although *The Eunuch* was not discovered until 1974. In the latter two works, the influence of Lastman is particularly noticeable.

When he returned to Leiden Rembrandt stayed in constant contact with another of Lastman's pupils, Jan Lievens (1607–74). The real extent of their collaboration is open to conjecture. Lievens, also a native of Leiden, was a year younger than Rembrandt but had begun painting earlier and we know that, at the very least, a healthy competitive spirit developed between the two young painters. They often worked on identical themes. In 1627 Rembrandt produced his *The Apostle Paul in Prison* (page 49), in 1628 *Peter*

Balaam and the Ass, *by Pieter Lastman, 1622.*
Oil on panel, 40.3 × 60.6 cm
Richard L. Feigen & Co, New York

and Paul in Conversation (Melbourne) and in 1629 *The Apostle Paul* (Nuremberg). At approximately the same time, Lievens painted the same apostle, seated in an armchair, quill in hand; the painting now hangs in Bremen. In 1631 rivalry between the two friends certainly helped to inspire their respective versions of The Crucifixion. Lievens' *Christ on the Cross* now hangs in the Musée des Beaux-Arts in Nancy; Rembrandt's composition on the same theme is also to be found in France, in the parish church of Le Mas d'Agenais (page 59). A comparison between these two

works reveals Lievens' closer affinity with Rubens, whereas Rembrandt has chosen a more personal approach, particularly in his humanizing of the Christ figure. In 1629, the two artists were visited by Constantijn Huygens (1596–1687), secretary to the Stadtholder. A man of letters, a musician and an amateur painter, Huygens was thoroughly conversant with several Italian, French and Dutch artists. As an enlightened art-lover for whom Rubens was a model of perfection, he was especially taken with Lievens, although he also admired Rembrandt, particularly

The Angel and the Prophet Balaam, *1626.*
Oil on canvas, 25 × 18 cm
Musée Cognacq-Jay, Paris

Self-Portrait, c.1629.
Pen and brown ink, 12.7 × 9.5 cm
The British Museum, London

Judas Returning the Thirty Pieces of Silver on which the artist was working at the time. Huygens was impressed by Judas's 'terrifying expression, his dishevelled hair, his torn clothing . . . the wretched man's entire body convulsed', which he contrasted to 'all the elegance of previous centuries'. He went on to compare Rembrandt and Lievens in these terms: 'I would make so bold as to pass a superficial judgement on these two. I must say that in the case of Rembrandt, he is superior on the level of taste and depth of feeling, whereas Lievens, for his part, dominates by virtue of a certain grandeur of invention and his analysis of subjects and characters.' Huygens urged both artists to visit Italy, a suggestion which neither ever followed up.

Around 1628–9 Rembrandt began work on his first self-portraits. Drawn around this time, a *Self-Portrait* in the British Museum already displays considerable authority of execution. The artist's lips are slightly parted and, as in the Rijksmuseum *Self-Portrait* (page 51), part of his face is masked in shadow. The freedom of line in both pen and grey-tinted brush strokes is admirable. A little later, Rembrandt produced an etching in which he presents himself as a *Laughing Beggar*. This individual style of self-portrayal is an expression of the artist's genuine sympathy with the humble and the poor.

We know that by July 1632 Rembrandt was living in Amsterdam although the precise date of his departure from Leiden is unclear. Commissions now began to pour in. In 1632, he was asked to paint a large portrait of the Amsterdam guild of surgeons, which is now known as *The Anatomy Lesson of Dr Tulp* (page 63). His arrival in Amsterdam coincided with a stylistic evolution. He began to work in a larger format, while bringing his characters closer to the observer's field of vision.

The Munich *Descent from the Cross* can be dated to approximately 1633; it is one of the first two panels in a series of five compositions on the Passion theme, commissioned by the Stadtholder Frederick Henry. The series was completed over a six-year period between 1633 and 1639. Rembrandt was aware of Rubens's *Descent* in Antwerp Cathedral, but his own version is less heroic, in that he uses his means of expression to create an image which is at once more human and more intensely religious. *The Resurrection* (page 85) belongs to this cycle.

Before he left Leiden, Rembrandt had already been in contact with the art dealer Hendrick van Uylenburgh. Once established in Amsterdam he became engaged to the latter's niece, Saskia van Uylenburgh, whose portrait he drew in silver-point (see page 16). The marriage took place in St Annaparochie, a small parish in Friesland, on 22 June 1634. Their first child,

The Descent from the Cross, *1633.*
Oil on panel, 93 × 68 cm
Alte Pinakothek, Munich

Rombartus, was born in December 1635, only to die in February of the following year. Only one of the four children born to Saskia and Rembrandt was to survive infancy.

Rembrandt was fascinated by the people he encountered in Amsterdam. In his earlier years he had been preoccupied by the study of forms, their power of expression and their relationship with light; he soon came to regard drawing as the best means of capturing a feeling, a sentiment or a thought. Many of his drawings are of scenes from daily life, either in his own family or in the world around him. He would

John the Baptist Preaching, c.1635.
Oil on canvas on wood, 62 × 80 cm
Berlin-Dahlem, Staatliche Museen Preussicher Kulturbesitz

sketch a whole range of characters on a single sheet of paper. Take the *Studies of Beggars and an Old Woman* which dates from between 1633 and 1634 (see page 15): here we have a study which gives equal value to the expressions of the beggars and to the people they are importuning. Then, in the centre of the composition, the artist places a child in tears, obviously abandoned to fend for himself.

It is generally agreed that *John the Baptist Preaching* (see page 14) was painted in about 1635. It possibly owes its origin to a preparatory black-and-white sketch for an etching, like the *Ecce Homo*. Using his favourite earth browns, Rembrandt was probably influenced by a composition by Lastman and also by a woodcut by J. Swart van Groningen, a sixteenth-century Dutch artist. All manner of people are seen listening to the prophet; some are fascinated, others indifferent, if not hostile. At the centre, the Pharisees are holding their own private, sinister conventicle. Meanwhile, in the rest of the picture, life goes on; mothers try to control their unruly children. Religion is the stuff of daily life. Rembrandt was particularly conscientious in the preparation of this work, leaving for posterity several preparatory sketches, the most notable of which is *Study of People in Conversation*. This is yet another example of the artist's interest in the study of expressions. Here the sketchiness of the broken line is not dissimilar to that in the unusual drawing of an *Elephant* (see page 17) of about 1637, in which Rembrandt brilliantly conveys the thickness of the animal's skin with a few deft touches. The drawing is wonderfully spontaneous and animated.

On 22 July 1638, a second child, Cornelia, was born to Rembrandt and Saskia. She too was to die in infancy on 13 August in the same year. A third child suffered the same fate in 1640. Only Titus, born in September 1640, was to survive. It was probably at some time between 1637 and 1640 that Rembrandt did his sketches depicting family life, among them the red ochre crayon composition entitled *Two Women Teaching a Child to Walk* (see page 17). With a few simple but emotionally charged strokes, the artist brings to life the everyday drama of two adults encouraging a child to take its first tentative steps.

Rembrandt had always been interested in the story of Samson. In 1636 he painted *The Blinding of Samson* (page 77). The artist's interest in the heroic and in pathos, his overwhelming passion, are themselves sufficient justification for the use of the term 'baroque'

Study of People in Conversation, *c.1635.*
Pen and brown ink, 19 × 12.5 cm
Staatliche Museen Preussicher Kulturbesitz, Berlin-Dahlem

Study of Beggars and an Old Woman, *c.1633–4.*
Pen and brown ink, 21.8 × 18.6 cm
Staatliche Museen Preussicher Kulturbesitz, Berlin-Dahlem

Saskia, *1633.*
Silver point on parchment, 18.5 × 10.7 cm
Staatliche Museen Preussicher Kulturbesitz, Berlin-Dahlem

An Elephant, c.1637.
Black chalk, 17.8 × 25.6 cm
British Museum, London

in relation to this painting and others of his youth, whereas his output during the 1640s was much calmer in a sense we might qualify as 'classical'. There is a danger, however, in drawing such oversimplified distinctions, since they tend to reduce his works to mere illustrations for some aesthetic theory.

Towards the end of the 1630s Rembrandt began to devote more attention to landscape, mostly in the form of drawings and etchings, using both media as a means to represent nature as he saw it. His paintings generally remained in the realm of the imaginary, with the possible exception of *Landscape with Stone Bridge* (page 79), which probably represents an actual location near Amsterdam.

On 5 January 1639, Rembrandt and Saskia took out a 13,000 florin mortgage, payable over six years, on a large house on St Anthoniesbreestraat, next door to Saskia's art-dealer uncle, Hendrick van Uylenburgh. They put down a deposit of a quarter of the total sum; the rest was to be repaid over five years. Rembrandt was to find the debt the cause of much financial trouble in future years, although at the time it did not seem an unreasonable expense in view of his success and his good prospects for the future.

It is curious that between 1634 and 1638 Rembrandt painted relatively few portraits; then, in the year 1639, there was a renewal of interest in him as a portrait painter. Several theories have been put forward to explain this. The earliest and most valid was suggested by an Italian writer on art, Baldinucci, in 1686: 'He must have received a large number of portrait commissions thanks to his reputation as a colourist which, we have to admit, was far in excess of his skills as a draughtsman. But when people realized that to have a portrait done by him involved sitting for as long as three months, candidates were few and far between.' On the other hand, another contemporary named Uytenbogaert said in his diaries that Rembrandt would do a portrait in a single day. These accounts need not be contradictory. Rembrandt could certainly paint large sections of the picture without the presence of a model, but it is also conceivable that for him portraiture represented two different kinds of painting: on the one hand, portraits concerned with physical features, or 'studies of expression', such as the paintings of friends or relatives which he would enjoy and complete comparatively

Two Women Teaching a Child to Walk, c.1640.
Red chalk, 10 × 12.5 cm
British Museum, London

Portrait of Baldassare Castiglione, after Raphael, *c.1639.*
Pen and brown ink, 16.3 × 20.7 cm
Graphische Sammlung Albertina, Vienna

---

quickly, and on the other, more developed and elaborate works. Moreover, Rembrandt's interest in history painting and teaching must have seriously limited his availability as a portrait artist. Perhaps his acquisition of a mortgage debt also accounts for his readiness to accept new commissions in 1639. He would certainly have needed to maintain a fairly high income to pay for the house.

On 9 April, Rembrandt attended an auction at which Raphael's *Portrait of Baldassarre Castiglione* (now in the Louvre) was put under the hammer. The fortunate

buyer was one Alfonso Lopez, a Spanish Jew in the Service of Cardinal Richelieu, who lived in Amsterdam between 1636 and 1640; he also owned an early Rembrandt, *The Angel and the Prophet Balaam* (see page 11). Rembrandt was very interested in Raphael's painting and made a quick sketch of it, *Portrait of Castiglione, after Raphael*. Rembrandt must have known Lopez personally, since Lopez owned another classic painting – Titian's *Portrait of a Man*, also known as *Portrait of Ariosto* (see page 20) – the composition of which, used in reverse, inspired an etched *Self-Portrait* by the artist in this same year; he used the same formula for a painted self-portrait the following year (page 89).

It is surprising that, in a Protestant country, Rembrandt should have accorded such importance to *The Death of the Virgin*, an apocryphal episode which he engraved in 1639. The young boy with a staff on the left of the work is clearly derived from Dürer's woodcut *The Death of the Virgin*; the descending angel may well have been inspired by *The Birth of the Virgin* by the same artist. It is known that Rembrandt bought two series of Dürer etchings at an auction in 1638: *The Life of the Virgin* and *The Passion*.

Titia, Saskia's closest sister, whose portrait Rembrandt painted in 1639, died in 1641. In September of the same year Saskia gave birth to a son, whom she called Titus in memory of her sister. Saskia herself died, probably of tuberculosis, on 14 June 1642. These were cruel times for Rembrandt who appears to have sought refuge in his own creations. In his private life he was uncertain. He engaged a servant, Geertge Dircx, to take care of Titus and lived with her for a while. In the midst of this emotional turbulence he nonetheless painted the great work we now know as *The Night Watch* (page 95).

In an engraving done in 1643, *The Three Trees* (see page 23), Rembrandt moved away from the usual naturalism of his landscapes. The ominous areas of light and shade are harbingers of a storm. Nevertheless, people are still going about their daily business. A tiny and insignificant figure sits drawing to the right of the scene, on the top of a dyke. Our attention is focused on the three trees. It is as if the wind from the sea has cleared away the clouds from around their branches. One is tempted to interpret their presence as an allusion to the three crosses on Calvary.

Self-Portrait, 1639.
Etching (second state), 20.5 × 16.2 cm
Petit Palais, Paris

In 1646, Rembrandt completed two additional paintings for the Passion series commissioned by the Stadtholder: *The Adoration of the Shepherds* (Munich) and *The Circumcision*, since lost. In the same year he also painted the charming little panel *Winter Landscape* which now hangs in the Kassel Museum in Germany.

Sometime during this period he made the etching *The Hundred Guilder Print*, generally considered to have been finished in 1649. The scene is taken from the Gospel according to St Matthew (19: 1–24). Jesus was in Judea and a large crowd had gathered: the Pharisees approached him, asking questions to test

Portrait of a Man
by Titian, c.1512.
Oil on canvas, 81.2 × 66.3 cm
National Gallery, London

The Artist Drawing at a Window, *1648.*
Etching (first state), 15.8 × 13 cm
Musée du Louvre, Paris

Beggars at the Door, *1648.*
Etching (first state), 16.4 × 12.8 cm
Musée du Louvre, Paris

him. Women brought their children to be touched by him only to be rebuffed by his disciples. Jesus said 'Suffer little children . . . to come unto me; for of such is the kingdom of heaven.' This is probably the moment Rembrandt sought to depict. To the right of the painting a group of sick people are beseeching Christ to heal them; to the left, the Pharisees are harassing him. Below them, in shadow, is a richly dressed young man, sitting listening to Christ. At the other end of the tableau a camel makes an appearance – a clear allusion to the parable 'it is easier for a camel to go through the eye of a needle than for a rich man to enter the kingdom of God.' The teachings of Jesus to his disciples, counselling them to renounce all

worldly goods, reinforced Rembrandt's conviction that the poor were probably closer to God. His drawings and engravings of this period are frequently peopled with the wretches he saw around him. *Beggars at the Door* of 1648 is a moving example. We are shown not just a solitary beggar, but an entire family asking for alms, dignified despite their misery. The woman, who is still young, is carrying a baby on her back and holds out her hand to the old man who, offering a coin, has an expression of genuine sympathy towards these people.

A moving self-portrait of 1648 represents *The Artist Drawing at a Window* (see page 21). The face is that of a man who has suffered. But this very suffering is determinedly offset by the strength of his creation. In October 1649, Geertge Dircx, Titus's nurse and Rembrandt's mistress, sued the painter for breach of promise of marriage. During the trial, Rembrandt's servant, Hendrickje Stoffels came to his defence. Geertge Dircx was awarded an annual pension of 200 guilders, although Rembrandt later had her sent to a house of correction. In about 1650 Hendrickje Stoffels took her place as housekeeper and mistress.

Between 1648 and 1652, Rembrandt paid at least two visits to Utrecht and Gelderland, staying in Amersfoort, not far from Utrecht. In *The View of the Singel at Amersfoort* (see page 24) he draws with such authority that the trunks and foliage of the trees bordering the canal to the left of the picture are achieved simply by a few strokes of the reed pen. The houses and the little bridge in the background are so precisely defined that the eye is led along the banks of the canal towards them. The white of the paper, a touch of wash and a few penstrokes to create reflections perfectly recreate the transparency of the water. This drawing can almost certainly be dated around 1648, whereas the *View of the Amstel at Amsterdam* (see page 25) must be a few years later. The houses and boats in the picture seem to be both a part of the river and separate from it. They are details which now appear of peripheral interest. The centre of the picture

is occupied by a small boat, as solitary as it is fragile. Here Rembrandt is at his peak, employing to the full his means of expression to translate the tranquil flow of water. His pen is at once rough and delicate, opaque and transparent, achieving a perfect rendition of the harmony between earth, water and sky with maximum of economy of means.

During this period Rembrandt made extensive use of the reed pen and, for his engravings, he cut directly into the copper with dry-point. An example of this is the *Cluster of Trees* of 1652 (see page 26). This technique exaggerates the dynamic of the line; one

The Three Trees, 1643.
Etching, 21.1 × 27.8 cm
Musée du Louvre, Paris

can feel the foliage rustling in the wind. At its first stage, which must have been observed from nature, the principal focus was the central wooden hut, half hidden by the trees. The strokes of the metal point are short, almost jerky, producing a wonderful effect of sunlight falling on the mass of the leaves. The white space to the right is left largely untouched, giving the picture an air of modernity.

View of the Singel at Amersfoort, *c.1648–50.*
Pen and brown ink, 15.2 × 27.7 cm
Musée du Louvre, Paris

View of the Amstel at Amsterdam, *c.1648–50.*
Pen and brown ink, 13.2 × 23.1 cm
Rijksmuseum, Amsterdam

Cluster of Trees, *1652.*
Dry point (second state), 12.4 × 21.1 cm
Petit Palais, Paris

Rembrandt's mounting financial problems came to a head in 1653 when he was obliged to take on new debts in order to pay off old ones. In July 1654, Rembrandt and Hendrickje were accused by the ecclesiastical court of living in sin. The girl admitted that she had 'surrendered herself to fornication with Rembrandt the painter'. She was 'punished, exhorted to do penance and excluded from the holy altar'. A few months later on 30 October, a baby daughter, Cornelia, was baptized at the Oude Kerk in Amsterdam. Rembrandt's two daughters with Saskia, both of whom died in infancy, had also been called Cornelia. The Church did not trouble Hendrickje about her supposed immorality after this time.

There is a fine drawing in the British Museum representing a *Woman Sleeping* (see page 28). Executed in a warm brown wash, it is probably contemporary with *Hendrickje Bathing* (page 109), painted in 1654.

The young woman yields to fatigue, resting her head on her arm, a virtuosity of brushstroke allowing the artist to suggest suppleness of forms with an admirable economy of means. On the other hand *The Three Crosses* (third state dated 1653), is a model of dramatic austerity. It is generally thought that the plate was reworked around 1660 and it is executed with dry-point and etcher's needle. On the right, those closest to Jesus are lamenting. The repentant executioner, pardoned by the Lord, dominates the group. To the left, a centurion with a tall headdress arrests the eye. Rembrandt borrowed the horseman's headgear from the medal of *Gian Francesco Gonzaga* by Pisanello and re-used it in *The Conspiracy of Julius*

View of the Amstel with Bathers, c.1655.
Pen and brown ink, 14.6 × 27.3 cm
Staatliche Museen Preussicher Kulturbesitz, Berlin-Dahlem

Civilis (page 129). In the preliminary states of the work, the figures were treated quite differently. By the fourth state the scene has been entirely modified. The dark areas are violently accentuated. A host of long vertical strokes combine to give the impression that all the dark forces of the Apocalypse are crashing down on Golgotha. The way in which Rembrandt simplifies his forms is such that one could almost describe his style as 'cubist'.

The application of geometric forms is to be found elsewhere in drawings of the same period, such as the *View of the Amstel with Bathers* in Berlin, dated around 1654–5.

Rembrandt seems to be playing with the very essence of drawing, that is to say with the relationship between line and the white of the paper. One of Rembrandt's students, Samuel van Hoogstraten, was doubtless recalling the words of his master when he advised the student of art to be 'miserly with all light

which is too intense and to let the paper act alone as much as possible'. The Amsterdam *Self-Portrait* (1655–6) is an example of Rembrandt's great delicacy in the use of the goose quill. Even so, the scratches in the paper are clearly visible in places, such was the intensity of the artist's pen-stroke. Rembrandt presents himself here wearing his painter's smock, hands on hips, as if defying posterity.

The drawing of *Butchers at Work* in Berlin (see page 30), has inevitably been compared with the painting in the Louvre dated 1655 (page 117). Benesch, writing about this kind of drawing, commented: 'the atmosphere seems to accumulate around the figures.' One is struck by the ordinary nature of the subject, the apparent awkwardness with which the figures are

A Woman Sleeping, *c.1655.*
Brush and brown wash, 24.5 × 20.3 cm
British Museum, London

Hendrickje Stoffels, *1660.*
Oil on canvas, 78.4 × 68.9 cm
Metropolitan Museum of Art, New York

Butchers at Work, c.1655.
Pen and brown ink, 13.4 × 17.9 cm
Staatliche Museen Preussicher Kulturbesitz, Berlin-Dahlem

presented. But Rembrandt captures the butchers at work as if they were weighing gold. The manner in which he depicts their labour is remarkable; they are stooped, immersed in their work. The powerful beast, quartered, reduced to flesh, constitutes the most luminous section of the scene. Flattened, dismembered, it represents a kind of *memento mori*. In this respect it shares the same spirit as the painting which is, in the words of Charles Sterling, 'a sordid interior illuminated by a bloody carcass. Dead meat retaining the extraordinary energy of life. A skinned ox transformed into the most precious pictorial material.'

Rembrandt's financial situation had scarcely improved. The proceeds of a sale of his goods in 1655 were insufficient to cover his debts. He signed over the deeds of his house to the chamber of orphans in the name of his son Titus, in order to avoid surrendering it to his creditors. In July 1656, Rembrandt was obliged to apply for *cessio bonorum* in the High

Court, which enabled him to declare himself 'honour-ably' bankrupt. The inventory of goods drawn up on 25–26 July by the auction room appraiser gives us a precious insight into the works Rembrandt had collected. Apart from his own paintings and drawings, the list includes works by Brouwer, Lievens, Seghers, Lastman, Porcellis and Jan Pynas along with the Italians (Palma Vecchio, Bassano, even Raphael). A series of antique busts is among the plaster-casts and there is all manner of exotic bric-à-brac including a Japanese helmet. A large collection of engravings includes examples by other Netherlandish artists, such as Lucas van Leyden, Brueghel, Goltzius, Muller and Heemskerk, and prints by Cranach, Schongauer, Dürer, F. Vanni and the Carracci. Among his collection of drawings there is mention of an album of landscapes by Savery. Rembrandt's own drawings are listed either in separate sheets, in lots or in ten volumes, organized according to subject matter. There is, for example, a volume of male and female nudes and three others which consist exclusively of landscapes. In purely quantitative terms, this inventory suggests that Rembrandt's collection of drawings may have amounted to about two thousand sheets.

In the same year, 1656, Rembrandt completed *The Anatomy Lesson of Dr Deyman* (see page 32). Like *The Anatomy Lesson of Dr Tulp* (page 63), this painting was hung in the anatomy amphitheatre in Amsterdam. It was almost completely destroyed during a fire in 1732, but a fragment survives. Deyman, who succeeded Nicolaes Tulp in 1653, was authorized to give his first anatomy lesson in 1656. Rembrandt's representation of the event is treated far more realistically than the *Lesson of Dr Tulp*, dealing vividly with the dissection of the skull. It is generally believed that the foreshortened perspective was inspired by Mantegna's *Dead Christ* (see page 33).

In 1657, Titus made a will in favour of Hendrickje and Cornelia, citing Rembrandt as usufructuary. Between 4 and 21 December of the same year, Rembrandt's paintings and other works of art were put up for auction; in February 1658, his house and furniture suffered the same fate; in September, his drawings and engravings were sold for a derisory sum. Titus, Hendrickje and Rembrandt set up home in a modest house in the Rozengracht in the Jordaan district of Amsterdam, which was largely populated by artisans and small shopkeepers. In 1660, Titus and Hendrickje formed a company employing Rembrandt and selling his paintings for him, thus protecting him from the usual legal requirements of bankruptcy.

Both *The Denial of St Peter* and the *Self-Portrait at the Easel* bear the date 1660. The following year, in 1661, Rembrandt received a commission to paint *The Conspiracy of Julius Civilis* (page 129). Since only part of the whole work remains, we must rely on a preliminary sketch (see page 35) to give us an indication of the overall design. Rembrandt's creative powers were still undiminished. He continued to accept portrait commissions such as the *Portrait of Jacob Trip* (National Gallery, London), painted in 1661. This is a study of an old, emaciated man, an immensely wealthy merchant of Dordrecht. However, Rembrandt no longer seeks to convey the prosperity and vigour of the successful merchant, as he would once have done. His subject is first and foremost a man near the end of his days. In 1662, Rembrandt painted his last great group portrait, *The Syndics of the Drapers' Guild* (page 131).

In 1653, the Sicilian nobleman, Don Antonio Ruffo had commissioned *Aristotle Contemplating the Bust of Homer* (page 107). In 1661, Rembrandt received another commission from the same source for *Alexander the Great*, the identity of which is uncertain, although arguments have been put forward for the *Man in Armour*, in Glasgow. Ruffo, enthusiastic about the earlier work, had reservations about his new purchase. Rembrandt enlarged the painting as he worked on it, leaving the stitches in the canvas clearly visible, which displeased his patron. Furthermore, Ruffo said that the portrait had cost him ten times as much as he would have paid for the work of a

The Anatomy Lesson of Dr Deyman, *1656.*
Oil on canvas, 100 × 134 cm
Rijksmuseum, Amsterdam

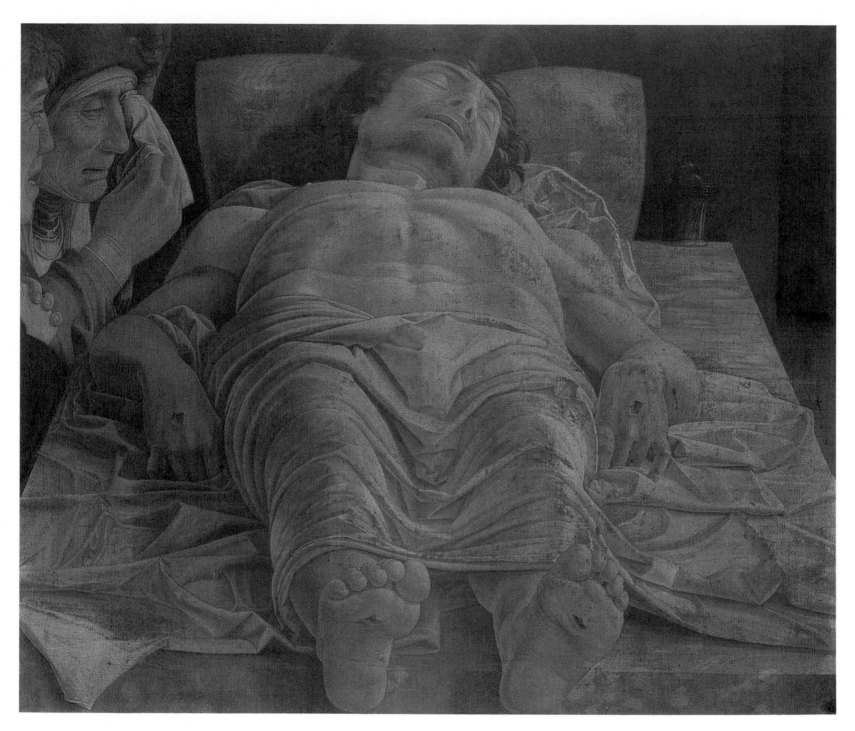

Lamentation over The Dead Christ.
by Andrea Mantegna, c.1500
Distemper on canvas, 68 × 81 cm
Pinacoteca di Brera, Milan

Homer, *1633.*
Oil on canvas, 100 × 82.5 cm
Mauritshuis, The Hague

contemporary Italian artist. Then in 1662 Rembrandt sent him *Homer Dictating to a Scribe* with which he was entirely dissatisfied and which he considered unfinished. Ruffo returned the painting to the artist demanding that he make adjustments to it. Rembrandt duly complied, dating the finished canvas 1663. From Ruffo's inventory we learn that the work included two scribes on the right, who were noting down the words of the old blind poet. The painting, which now hangs in The Hague, has been damaged by fire and the right-hand section cut out, but from an early sketch in Stockholm we can reconstruct the original design. Homer's face has the same features which appeared in *Aristotle Contemplating the Bust of Homer* (page 107). We are not able to identify it from the sketch because the lines are merely schematic, providing only a general indication of the overall composition. Even so, this is more than enough to convey the fascination that the poet's words are exercising over the young scribe. The disposition of light is masterful. Homer is drawn in half-light and, as in the painting, face and shoulder are indirectly lit. The pen strokes are transformed on the canvas into broad, flat surfaces of paint. The colours are powerful but muted, softening the intensity of the luminous contrasts. The character of Homer, like that of St Paul, fascinated Rembrandt in his later years. One is inevitably tempted to see something of the ageing artist in this portrait, a close affinity between Rembrandt and the blind poet, hands outstretched in the delivery of an oration.

Hendrickje Stoffels died in July 1663. Despite this bereavement, Rembrandt continued to paint. Although nineteenth-century opinion tended to suggest that by this time in his life Rembrandt was largely neglected, this is not entirely true. On 29 December 1667, for example, the publisher Pieter Blaeu brought Cosimo de' Medici to visit him. On 28 February 1668, Titus van Rijn married Magdalena van Roo in the Nieuwe Kerk of Amsterdam but he died in September of the same year. His posthumous daughter, Titia, was baptized on 22 March 1669. On 4

Homer Dictating to a Scribe, c.1663.
Pen and brush with brown wash, 14.5 × 16.7 cm
Nationalmuseum, Stockholm

October, Rembrandt himself died at the age of sixty-three. An inventory of his possessions reveals that he had managed to assemble a new collection of works of art. He was buried on 8 October in the Westerkerk, as Hendrickje and Titus had been.

European art in the seventeenth century was, on the whole, supported by the Church and the aristocracy. But in the Dutch Republic, an artist's living often came either in the form of commissions from the upper middle classes or from sales on the art market. This meant that Rembrandt never enjoyed the security of continuous patronage. In this sense, he was more able to follow the dictates of his own taste than were many of his contemporaries. It also meant, such was the breadth and generosity of his vision, that even at the end of his life he enjoyed only partial recognition; the freedom of expression he permitted himself was clearly out of step with the predominant attitudes of the time. It was only Rembrandt's disciples who began to spread his style and, indeed, to posit valid criticism of his work.

A Model in the Artist's Studio, *c.1655.*
Pen and grey wash, 20.5 × 19 cm
Ashmolean Museum, Oxford

Rembrandt sought to teach his pupils not only certain techniques, but also certain attitudes towards art. Early in his career he set up a studio in Leiden where, from 1628, he taught Gerrit Dou. In Amsterdam, from 1632 to 1635, Rembrandt stayed with the art dealer Hendrick Uylenburgh, who had founded an academy of sorts. This contact with Uylenburgh probably served to focus Rembrandt's ideas about the organization of his teaching. In many ways he broke with the traditional corporate rules of the city. The guilds had perpetuated the medieval organization of studios, which allowed only certain apprentices to study with a master. Rembrandt's notion of the academy, on the other hand, was derived from the system employed by the Mannerists of Haarlem who, in turn, had borrowed their ideas from the Italian Renaissance. Rembrandt's teaching was simple: drawing was of the utmost importance. For him, one of the best ways of learning was to observe and draw existing works of art or models. Thus his students were encouraged to draw from engravings, paintings or antique objects. In fact, Rembrandt's own works were amongst the first to be copied. But he also encouraged working with live models, as we can see in a drawing by one of his pupils entitled *Rembrandt's Studio with Female Model*. We know that Rembrandt rented a house on the Bloemgracht which he converted into small individual studios to enable his students to concentrate better on their subjects and to encourage them to develop their individual talents.

Joachim von Sandrart, a German artist and historian, definitely knew Rembrandt when he lived in Amsterdam between 1637 and 1641. The author of *Teutsche Academie*, published in 1675–79, he reports that Rembrandt had innumerable students in his workshop, paying an annual fee of 100 florins. It is hard to guess what Sandrart meant by 'innumerable', but the number may have been in excess of twenty. One wonders also just who these artists attending the workshop were. We know of Gerbrand von Eeckhout, who worked in the master's studio in the late 1630s, and became a great friend. Sometime between

The Conspiracy of Julius Civilis, *1661.*
Pen and ink with brown wash, 19.6 × 18 cm
Staatliche Graphische Sammlung, Munich

1635 and 1640 two artists who were later to become famous attended Rembrandt's classes: Govaert Flinck and Ferdinand Bol. Samuel van Hoogstraten and Nicholaes Maes studied with him later, towards the end of the 1640s. Aert de Gelder was one of his last disciples working with him around 1660.

Rembrandt's work has sometimes been greeted, in his own country and abroad, with a certain amount of circumspection. Sandrart was particularly severe, criticizing the master for disregarding the basic rules of art, particularly with respect to anatomy, proportion and perspective. Rembrandt's student, Samuel van Hoogstraten, published in 1678 the *Inleyding tot de Hooge Schoole der Schilderkonst*, in which he raises the example of *John the Baptist Preaching*. He professes to be shocked by the presence of two dogs coupling – a possible allusion to the wickedness of the

Self-Portrait, 1669.
Oil on canvas, 86 × 70.5 cm
National Gallery, London

Self-Portrait, *by Edgar Degas, c.1857–8.*
Oil on paper mounted on canvas, 26 × 19 cm
Sterling and Francine Clark Art Institute,
Williamstown, Massachusetts

Pharisees – considering this detail to be trivial. He criticizes such scenes, which 'reveal the master's naïvety' saying 'they are even more ridiculous in that they are not even very well observed'. This reaction is symptomatic of the 'classicizing' tendency that was increasingly prevalent in the Netherlands.

In general, his etchings were well received, especially in France and Italy. The paintings met with a mixed reception, as we know from the reaction of Don Antonio Ruffo. On the other hand, Louis XIV of France included *Self-Portrait at the Easel* in the royal collection. Rembrandt's drawings were widely coveted by seventeenth-century collectors. In 1686, Baldinucci spoke of Rembrandt with the greatest respect, pointing to the high value placed on them. The French critic, Roger de Piles, in his *Abrégé de la vie des peintres* (1699), compared Rembrandt with Raphael, as Sandrart had done; refusing to accept the former as a history painter, he considered his art to be a reflection of the 'native character of his country'. Roger de Piles also owned a large number of Rembrandt drawings.

Real interest in Rembrandt began to grow in the second half of the eighteenth century. In 1742, Louis XV purchased *The Angel Raphael Leaving the Family of Tobias* (Musée de Lille) which was frequently copied in the nineteenth century, most notably by Delacroix. Boucher owned a series of Rembrandt drawings and acquired the Fragonard copy of *The Holy Family* (1645). Fragonard himself continued to be influenced by the warmth and intensity of light in Rembrandt's work throughout his life. But for most French, Italian and German artists of the eighteenth century – Chardin and Piazzetta, for example – Rembrandt's influence was not great.

It was not until the end of the century that an artist emerged who had profound affinities with Rembrandt. Goya claimed that, nature apart, he had two masters: Velázquez and Rembrandt. This admission, and the direct correspondences between Goya's *Self-*

Portrait of 1815 and Rembrandt's later self-portraits underline the extent to which the two artists are related. Their common capacity for introspection brings them together; their respective portraits explore the essential secret of man. They capture the revelations inherent in the fleeting expression of a moment, adding the signs of character evident in the sitter's pose, clothes and gestures to complete the portrait. In his peaceful republic, Rembrandt delved into the human soul, accepted its weaknesses and let us know what he thought about it. In the war-torn kingdom of Spain, Goya was appalled by the unfathomable barbarity in the hearts of men, but his response, through his painting, was an indomitable celebration of life. This kind of brotherhood, existing as it does outside time and space, stems from a shared acceptance of life as it comes, from an ability to live that life with the utmost sincerity.

In England, Reynolds studied Rembrandt closely, and his landscapes influenced artists of the Norwich School, particularly Crome. In France he was to be greatly admired by the Romantics; Delacroix's *Assassination of the Bishop of Liège*, for instance, is a homage to the master. But often the very esteem in which he was held engendered misconceptions. Rembrandt was popularly perceived as the misunderstood genius. His critical reputation laboured under the weight of cliché right up to the beginning of the twentieth century. Fromentin's criticism of *The Anatomy Lesson of Dr Tulp*, for example, is a masterpiece of misunderstanding – Dutch painting seen through the lens of 'realism'. He also considered Rembrandt's output almost exclusively in terms of light and shade. Even if we accept that means often become ends, we should not lose sight of the fact that chiaroscuro was, for Rembrandt, only a technique, however masterfully exploited, designed to attract the attention of the observer. The eye is seized by the intensity of the luminous contrasts which emphasize the most expressive areas in a scene or a figure. As Rembrandt grew older, his vision intensified and he reduced the contrasts in order to guide the observer's perception directly to the essence of the work. This is far from being the pure realism often thought to categorize Dutch art. When Gustave Courbet visited the Netherlands in 1846, he particularly admired *The Night Watch*, and two of his works, *Burial at Ornans* and *The Departure of the Firemen*, can be seen as an echo of Rembrandt's great composition. Jean-François Millet certainly felt closer to Rembrandt than Fromentin did, most noticeably in his choice of themes. He was impressed by some of Rembrandt's etchings, such as *The Holy Family* (1654) and those scenes representing the lives of beggars. The painter and print-maker Odilon Redon was a great admirer of the light and shade in Rembrandt's etchings, and during his first visit to Holland, in July 1868, standing in front of *The Night Watch* (page 95), he could be heard murmuring: 'Magic, that's the word – the quality of light is fairy-like and supernatural'.

The Slaughtered Ox in the Louvre (page 117) was to inspire many artists, including the German painter Lovis Corinth in 1892 and 1893. More surprising perhaps is the keen interest shown by Edgar Degas in Rembrandt's work. In his beautiful self-portrait as a youth, known as *Degas in a Soft Hat* (see page 39), his use of light is derived directly from Rembrandt's portraits. Degas' later monotypes are a clear expression of his interest in the great Dutch painter's chiaroscuro. Finally, we should certainly mention that Picasso was also influenced by Rembrandt, particularly in the period between 1967 and 1971 when he used *St Paul* (Stuttgart) and *Danaë* in the Hermitage (page 101) as sources of inspiration.

Art is not simply a question of talent. We can admire Raphael for the beauty of his forms; but while he might help us to learn how to draw he does not always touch our hearts. Art must take hold of the observer and carry him outside himself. The French painter Eugène Delacroix felt this instinctively, daring to turn the traditional hierarchy on its head by saying: 'Perhaps one day people will realize that Rembrandt is a much greater painter than Raphael.'

Rembrandt's goals, his personal and artistic aims, must remain a matter of hypothesis and conjecture. However, one can learn a great deal by considering the function of the image. For Poussin the image was, above all else, a form of speech. One is tempted to think that Rembrandt saw the image primarily as a reflection of his emotions, of his vision, and of his faith. Rembrandt's works are an essential revelation of the artist's inner self. His career was a history of internal struggle, a never-ending battle to remain resolute in the face of adversity.

If Rembrandt concerned himself with humanity, he did so more as a psychologist than an anatomist. Appearances are only important in so far as we can guess what lies concealed behind them. Rembrandt did not hide from reality; he did not shrink from portraying the indelicate or ugly.

The artist protected his creative powers from the menace of the world by a constant expression of profound sympathy for the men and women around him. It was this generosity of spirit towards others which allowed him to reach for the essential in his pictorial representation of them. This sense of juggling with the ephemeral to achieve the universal gives Rembrandt his timeless quality.

Even now his works have an astonishing contemporaneity. There are many reasons for this, the most important being the challenge he set himself in his youth: to be constantly more 'himself'. And this self was invested with a charity which, though based in religion, was no less a product of his essential humanity. Like Velázquez, Rembrandt did not hesitate to portray the infirm and the deformed, lowly servant girls and beggars. This is what makes Rembrandt's genius universal. But the determining factor will always be the intensity and absolute sincerity with which he viewed the world. Rembrandt had learned to find meaning both within himself and outside himself and lived his life with a corresponding degree of spiritual intensity.

1606 ❧ 1669

THE PLATES

In this picture, dated 1625, the earliest that can be attributed without doubt to Rembrandt, the artist made his debut as a history painter.

Chosen with six others to celebrate the faith, Stephen 'did great wonders and miracles among the people'. He was arrested by members of the synagogue, condemned, and flung from the city to be executed. 'And they stoned Stephen, calling upon God and saying "Lord Jesus, receive my spirit". And he kneeled down and cried with a loud voice, "Lord, lay not this sin to their charge".' (Acts, 7: 59–60.)

Rembrandt convincingly projects the group hysteria which can turn false witnesses into torturers, and he has the humility, or vanity, to give one of them his own face. His self-portrait appears just above St Stephen's head. The composition is derived from those Utrecht painters who had been influenced by Caravaggio. A frontal plane to the left lies bathed in shadow, concealing a turbanned man who reins in a nervous horse, and acts as a foil to the brightly lit area in which the action unfolds. The man seated in the background with garments in his lap, surrounded by attendants, represents Saul – the future St Paul – who consented to the death and dealt ruthlessly with the Christians before his conversion.

The Stoning of St Stephen

Painted 1625
89.5 × 123.6 cm
Musée des Beaux-Arts, Lyon

Like nearly all the master's works of this period, this picture is painted on a wooden panel. The subject is drawn from the Book of Tobit. Tobit was an Israelite renowned for honesty, goodness and generosity, who was blinded. No longer able to provide for himself, one day Tobit heard his wife return from her day's labour with a kid which she had been given. Thinking that she must have stolen the animal he begged her to return it. Whereupon 'She replied . . . "Where are thine alms and thy righteous deeds? Behold, thou and all thy works are known".' (Tobit, 2: 11–14.) In despair Tobit then implored God to remember him.

The old man seated near the hearth seems caught at the moment when, aggrieved at being insulted, he begins praying that God should end his life. No doubt Rembrandt draw inspiration from the pictures on this theme by Bloemaert and Buytewech. Buytewech's etching demonstrates a desire for simultaneous balance and contrast: for example, a fire in the background separates the protagonists. Rembrandt, on the other hand, moves the fire to the foreground to create a diagonal axis which separates the couple without placing them in opposition. The aged Tobit prays to God, his once sumptuous clothes now patched. His wife looks on in astonishment at the consequences of her reproach. A little dog, symbolizing wedded fidelity, lies at Tobit's feet to banish any uncertainty as to their deeper feelings.

Rembrandt makes certain mistakes attributable to youthful inexperience. We might wonder, for example, how the roof is attached to the wall in which the window is found. Yet he demonstrates great facility in his use of light. To the two visible sources of illumination, the fire and the window, he has added a third which seems to fall diagonally from our left, throwing the two figures into sharp relief.

Anna Accused by Tobit of Stealing the Kid

Painted 1626
40.1 × 29.9 cm
Rijksmuseum, Amsterdam

Throughout his life, Rembrandt was fascinated by St Paul, whose life and work reflected a profound and passionate soul. Saul the Pharisee who had overseen the stoning of St Stephen and persecuted the early Christians was 'seized by Jesus Christ' on the road to Damascus. Paul was introduced to the apostles as a convert. Highly educated and untiring, he carried Christ's teachings throughout the Near East, as the principal author of the Acts of the Apostles and thirteen Epistles. Hence he is traditionally portrayed with books and a sword – the weapon by which he was to die – which Rembrandt is careful not to omit.

The clear colours of the preceding picture have grown darker, while the light has also become more concentrated and its source more explicit. The apostle is seen meditating while in captivity, and this iconography seems completely original. Light from the left illuminates the cell through the bars of the window, and the contrast between the cell and the contemplation in which the saint is steeped is striking. The artist has signed and dated the work – 1627 – in the open book. The following year he executed a picturing showing *St Peter and St Paul in Conversation* (Melbourne), while around 1629–30 he was to draw and engrave another *St Paul Meditating* (Louvre, Paris).

The Apostle Paul in Prison

Painted 1627

72.8 × 60.3 cm

Staatsgalerie, Stuttgart

Rembrandt is about twenty-two here. A young artist, scarcely established, is painting himself. Whereas another might have sought to reproduce his own features as exactly as possible, Rembrandt chooses to use a side light which illuminates his face indirectly. Only his neck and cheek are clearly visible; the nose and mouth are barely distinguishable while the eyes can be made out in half-shadow. His tousled hair does nothing to suggest any concern to leave a flattering image for posterity. Using an original technique, he has underscored the hair's unruliness with the handle of the paintbrush, enhancing the portrait's spontaneous feel. Yet above all it is the expertise and technique which impress. Usually the face is one of the best lit areas of a painted portrait. Here, in complete contrast, the man is no longer a face but has himself become a shadow, standing out against a wall of light, in which a blend of green and white paint suggests a translucent surface.

Another *Self-Portrait*, in Munich, which appears to have been painted a little later, is dated 1629. A drawn *Self-Portrait* again shows a young man half in shadow (see page 11). These self-portraits constitute a category on their own. Why produce a self-portrait? Was the young Rembrandt seeking to assert himself by painting his own image? Or was he attempting to capture a fleeting moment? This, and a lively desire to examine every aspect of the human condition – which his interest in the poor confirms – bear witness to his generosity of spirit and understanding of humanity.

Self-Portrait

Painted c.1628
22.6 × 18.7 cm
Rijksmuseum, Amsterdam

In the foreground one of the pilgrims has flung himself at Christ's feet, overturning a chair. Christ rises up in the light like some prophetic vision. Together they form a great diagonal which dominates the composition. The second pilgrim shrinks from the revelation to which he is a witness. Rembrandt uses the strongly lit table to reflect light back on to the protagonists and draw attention to the tall silhouette standing out against a dazzling expanse of wall.

In his *Self-Portrait* (page 51) Rembrandt had already exploited the same technique of strongly lighting one area, against which a face or silhouette stands out. This derives from Caravaggio, as does the figure of the pilgrim in the foreground. We should remember that Terbrugghen had returned from Italy in 1614, and Honthorst in 1620, and that they made a deep impression on such young Dutch artists as Lievens and, in a different way, Rembrandt. It is also possible to detect here the influence of the German Adam Elsheimer, another visitor to Italy. An engraving of one of his pictures, *Philemon and Baucis*, may have inspired certain elements of Rembrandt's composition, for example the Christ figure.

Christ at Emmaus

Painted c.1629
37.4 × 42.3 cm
Musée Jacquemart-André, Paris

An old man, bearing a resemblance to the many old men that Rembrandt drew, painted or engraved at this period, has just escaped from the burning city. Richly dressed but barefoot, he rests and meditates, while beside him lie the objects he has saved from the catastrophe: a few pieces of precious metal and a Bible. The light draws our eyes to the bottom left of the painting, then flows diagonally up along the outline of Jeremiah and finally illuminates the prophet's face in a more subtle fashion. The dominant colours are greys and ochres. The diagonal of Jeremiah's body is articulated by the reddish-brown of the fur, the grey cloak and the green tunic. To render the gold embroidery on the carpet and the metalwork, Rembrandt used encrustations of paint which catch the light.

A possible contemporary influence on this painting is the figure of St Peter in Guido Reni's *The Apostles Peter and Paul*, painted at the beginning of the century. In his own manner Rembrandt has transformed the image of Melancholy into a biblical figure.

The Prophet Jeremiah Lamenting the Destruction of Jerusalem

Painted 1630
58.3 × 46.6 cm
Rijksmuseum, Amsterdam

Using huge flagstones, grandiose temple architecture apparently half-emptied of the faithful, and several beggars who draw near, in curiosity, to a group of three kneeling adults, Rembrandt composes the elements of his scene in masterly fashion. The vanishing point is placed slightly to the left, outside the picture. One's glance rests a moment at the right on the two seated old men: at the centre Joseph and his two doves remain in darkness. A ray of light focuses attention on the shoulders and raised right hand of the prophetess Anna, and lingers on the kneeling Virgin and on Simeon, who calls on heaven as witness and clasps the child in his arms.

The Holy Spirit had told Simeon, a 'just and devout' man, that he would not die before he had seen the Christ. Now, he arrives at the Temple of Jerusalem at the moment when Jesus' parents are bringing their son to be 'purified' according to the Law of Moses. Receiving the Child in his arms, Simeon prophesies to his mother that he will have a great destiny (Luke, 2: 22–38).

A comparison with a *Simeon in the Temple*, which hangs in Hamburg and was executed around 1627–28, clearly shows the artist's development. Here he abandons the kind of frontal frieze-like view derived from Lastman, and uses light in a different way: it no longer illuminates a wall behind the figures, but lights them directly. The picture is small in dimensions, but the intended effect is obtained – a grandiose setting creates a monumental composition.

The Presentation in the Temple

Painted 1631
60.9 × 47.8 cm
Mauritshuis, The Hague

In the same year that Rembrandt created *The Pre-sentation in the Temple* (page 57), he executed a *Christ on the Cross*, which is now in the church of Le Mas d'Agenais, on the Garonne, not far from Marmande. The work appears to be the result of a kind of contest between Rembrandt and his colleague Lievens, for a very similar composition by Lievens, also arched, of comparable dimensions and dated 1631, is in the museum at Nancy.

A healthy rivalry inspired the two artists. When Rembrandt drew and engraved his *St Paul Meditating* of 1629–30, Lievens was also painting the same subject. It may be that they had both been given the same commission, in competition with each other; Rembrandt and Lievens certainly painted their versions of the Crucifixion at the same time. Both removed the figures usually seen around the cross so that Jesus appears alone at the point of death. In Lievens' *Christ* blood flows abundantly from the wound, and the closed eyes and half-open mouth leave little room for hope. By contrast Rembrandt's figure does not appear yet to have given up the ghost. His suffering seems unbearable, but a body radiant with light and a sky in which the clouds are parting add another dimension.

Christ on the Cross

Painted 1631
99.9 × 72.6 cm
Parish church of Le Mas d'Agenais, Lot et Garonne

This portrait of a wealthy Amsterdam merchant was completed while Rembrandt was planning his move to that city and paying regular visits, before finally settling there at the end of 1631. Nicolaes Ruts' father had made a fortune in trade and founded a company with links abroad, notably with Russia. This may explain the fur cloak and hat.

The figure is seen at an angle, but turns his face directly towards the spectator. He is silhouetted against a light coloured wall. The right hand rests on the back of a chair and is painted in a slightly clumsy manner reminiscent of hands in portraits by Lievens. In contrast Ruts' left hand, which holds out a note bearing Rembrandt's monogram, is better modelled. The features are appropriate to a man of fifty-eight bearing many responsibilities.

Portrait of Nicolaes Ruts

Painted 1631
116.8 × 87.3 cm
Frick Collection, New York

We are present at a private demonstration of dissection, presided over by the renowned Nicolaas Tulp (1593–1674). After studying in Leiden under Pieter Pauw, himself a pupil of Vesalius, Tulp returned to Amsterdam where he was appointed professor in 1629. It may well be that this patron heard talk in Lieden of the growing reputation of a young painter native to the town. Indeed, there is other evidence to suggest that the intellectual elite which had been educated in Leiden helped Rembrandt after his arrival in Amsterdam, by passing important commissions on to him. Generally regarded as the most eminent anatomist in the United Provinces, Tulp had built the Theatrum Anatomium. His first two public lectures were given in January 1631 and January 1632.

Rembrandt's picture undoubtedly shows the second of these, in which Professor Tulp explains the function of the muscles of the left arm, using the body of an executed criminal. As Frans Hals did in his own manner, Rembrandt raised the group portrait to the level of history painting. He succeeded in holding the spectator's attention while presenting a group of figures most of whom are not looking at the artist.

Fromentin disliked this picture, criticizing the corpse, which he saw as no more than 'a pale lighting effect in a black picture'. He concludes his case thus: Rembrandt's 'subject was a man, he was not concerned with the human form; his subject was death, and he overlooked it in order to search his palette for a whitish tone representing light.' The response to such criticism is simple. Throughout his life Rembrandt found little interest in the physical beauty of the human figure, despite advising his pupils to train themselves through academic studies. He himself studied Mantegna in order to grasp that artist's ability to establish a relationship between form and space, and not for the forms themselves.

The Anatomy Lesson of Dr Tulp

Painted 1632
169.5 × 216.5 cm
Mauritshuis, The Hague

To Rembrandt's eyes the corpse here was only a container deserted by the soul, and Fromentin was right to say that Rembrandt did not paint death. Throughout his career Rembrandt explored in paintings and drawings the links between man and death, but it was man's struggle, not his capitulation, to which he drew attention.

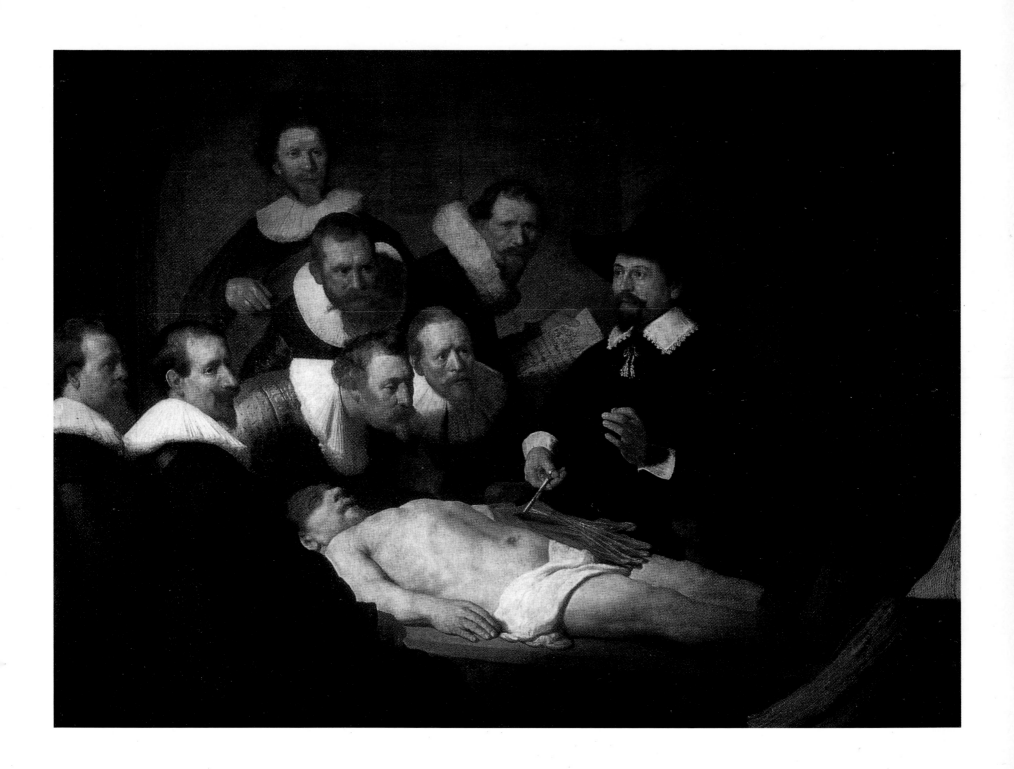

The oak panel on which this study of a *Man in Oriental Costume* is painted was originally rectangular. In *The Anatomy Lesson of Dr Tulp* (page 63) Rembrandt had proved himself a great portrait painter; here he reveals his fascination for mood studies, combined with an attraction towards oriental exoticism. The man, in his middle years, has an authoritarian air; the staff in his hand and the rich eastern costume reinforce this impression. The plumed and bejewelled turban and the crescent earring heighten both his 'Turk of the Bazaar' side and his powerful personality.

What is it that so fascinates us in this picture? Is it the figure's pose, with the right arm raised high? Or the light on his cloak which cuts an oval frame around the profile, in which the colours start to lighten and glow as one draws nearer to the face? Or even the green and gold tones which bewitch us? Nobody can deny the virtuosity of the artist in this handsome rendering of the figure's dress and his masculine power. We should remember that in June 1633 Rembrandt was betrothed to Saskia, and that the number of self-portraits he completed in that year is evidence of his new assurance.

Man in Oriental Costume

Painted 1633
85.8 × 63.8 cm
Alte Pinakothek, Munich

Rembrandt painted a number of compositions with mythological themes shortly before and after his marriage to Saskia van Uylenburgh in 1633. Around 1631 he engraved a *Diana Bathing*, and the following year an *Abduction of Europa*. Then in 1635 he completed *The Abduction of Ganymede*. After this time, works with obviously mythological subjects became more rare.

There may be various reasons why he was attracted to such themes at this particular point. His arrival in Amsterdam probably constituted something of a break from the pious atmosphere of his own family. His marriage into an important Frisian family probably inspired him to paint the kind of mythological pictures which were valued by the aristocracy.

Here the stories of Callisto and of Actaeon, as told in Ovid's *Metamorphoses*, have been daringly linked together. A group of nymphs are frolicking in the water. One of them, in the centre, turns idly to the right. Others are scrambling on to the bank to join the nymphs attacking the unfortunate Callisto. She has been seduced by Zeus and is unable to hide the fact that she is pregnant. From the young nymph in the foreground another diagonal leads to Diana, recognizable from the crescent moon in her hair. She is turning towards the hunter Actaeon, whose discovery of the goddess eventually leads to his being turned into a stag and devoured by his own hounds.

The nudes in this picture do not conform to the classical ideal. Their expressions are more human than divine and establish links between the different groups. The light draws our attention to the water and the nude bodies, while the presence of Actaeon half in shadow is not immediately obvious. Even so, behind him the dark forest opens on to a distant prospect. The clear tones of this vista counterbalance the diagonal of milky flesh formed by the nymphs on the right of the picture.

Diana and her Nymphs Bathing, with Actaeon and Callisto

Painted c.1634
73.5 × 93.5 cm
Museum Wasserburg Anholt, Anholt

This could almost be called a drawing rather than a painting. Its dimensions are those of a *modello* and the oil paint has been applied to paper which was then stuck on to canvas.

The work is a preparation for an etching but its interest lies neither in its function nor its mechanics. For in this work Rembrandt resumes his concern with the stories of the Bible and with humanity. It is notable that the figure of Christ is less detailed than certain others. In Rembrandt's vision, Christ is the object of debate but remains outside it. He draws with evident enthusiasm the different postures of the high priests demanding Jesus's death. One calms the crowd with a gesture of his hand, another kneels at Pilate's feet to seize the commander's baton; another, slightly behind, holds his hand to his heart in a sign of good faith, while two of his more agitated colleagues hurl abuse at Pontius Pilate, who tries to escape. Behind them the soldiers, looking more like Batavian than Roman troops, seem confused and astonished at the crowd's ferocity.

Christ before Pilate and the People

Painted 1634
54.5 × 44.5 cm
National Gallery, London

Maerten Soolmans (1613–41), whose family were natives of Antwerp, studied in Leiden before marrying Oopjen Coppit in 1633. She was two years older than him and a member of an aristocratic Amsterdam family – her portrait, now in a private collection in Paris, is the counterpart to that shown here. The two pictures were certainly marriage portraits, which explains the ostentatious richness of the couple's clothing.

Full-length and life-size, they demonstrate the extraordinary mastery of portraiture that Rembrandt had now attained. The placing of the hand, foot and curtain heightens the sensation of a slight movement to the right. Oopjen turns towards the left, but the two newly-weds are approaching each other while watching the painter. The fine execution of the face and lacework would certainly have delighted the sitters.

Here Rembrandt has successfully orchestrated a symphony of blacks. If it were not for the face, slightly coarsened for his age, we might take the subject for a Spanish grandee, a somewhat provocative comparison, but one that makes us appreciate how the bourgeois figure, whose single-mindedness has brought him freedom and fortune, found in Rembrandt a portraitist equal to his ambitions.

Portrait of Maerten Soolmans

Painted 1634
209.8 × 134.8 cm
Private Collection

A young woman decked out in eastern costume – perhaps borrowed from a theatre – garlanded with flowers, holds a staff twined about with foliage in her right hand. Historians have debated whether this is the portrait of a specific young woman – several see Saskia here – or of Flora, goddess of flowers and the spring.

It is difficult to say whether this slightly strained face with its cheerful but veiled expression represents Saskia. Like Rubens after him, Rembrandt tended to approximate the features of the women he painted to those of his wife. The recently noted similarity between Flora's pose and that of the wife of Giovanni Arnolfini in Jan van Eyck's *Arnolfini Marriage* (National Gallery, London) seems convincing on all points. The prominent stomach and the left hand resting on it appear very similar.

This work belongs to the series of mythological paintings completed by Rembrandt in the years 1633–35. The artist took up the theme again in 1635 in a canvas now in The National Gallery, London, entitled *Flora*, this time showing the model in three-quarter face and offering a posy.

Saskia (?) as Flora

Painted 1634
124.7 × 100.4 cm
The Hermitage, St Petersburg

A banquet becomes a drama. King Belshazzar stands frozen at the sight of an inscription, which a mysterious disembodied hand is tracing on the wall. The meal is interrupted, goblets are turned over and the assembled guests are terrified. Belshazzar was giving a magnificent feast, in the course of which vessels of gold and silver were brought to him which his father, Nebuchadnezzar, had taken from the sanctuary in Jerusalem. Suddenly a hand wrote an incomprehensible message on the wall. None of the wise men could decipher it until Daniel succeeded in interpreting its significance – Belshazzar's downfall (Daniel, 5–6).

This Old Testament subject had only rarely been painted before Rembrandt, although he may have been inspired by P. de Grebber's composition of 1625. The woman seen from the back who blocks off the composition at the right was taken from Veronese's *Abduction of Europa* (Doge's Palace, Venice), which Rembrandt could have known through a variant in Amsterdam. In 1639 Rembrandt was to draw inspiration from Veronese yet again when he made the portrait of Titia van Uylenburgh, his sister-in-law (Stockholm). The scene is given a particularly dynamic force by the two diagonals formed by the table and Belshazzar. It is dominated by the figure of the latter who supports himself on the table, while the light which illuminates the guests and leaves the musicians in shadow seems to derive from the inscription itself.

Belshazzar's Feast

Painted c.1635
167.6 × 209.2 cm
National Gallery, London

In a letter dated 27 January 1639, Rembrandt asked Constantin Huygens to accept a canvas, very probably this picture, advising him in a postscript to hang it in a strongly lit position so that it could be seen from some distance away.

The popular biblical hero Samson was pursued by the Philistines. His superhuman strength was equalled only by his weakness for women. Delilah determined to betray him and eventually he told her that his strength resided in his long hair. Having sent him to sleep she cut off his hair; the Philistines 'took him, and put out his eyes, and brought him down to Gaza' (Judges, 16: 4–21).

Artists more usually represented Delilah cutting Samson's hair. Rembrandt chose a more violent moment, when the soldiers are blinding him. At least three diagonals, formed by the soldiers on the right, the hero's right leg, and the lance carried by the soldier on the left, point towards Samson's face. The somewhat cowardly soldier on the left stands out against the light which turns his clothes a purplish hue. The weapons, chain and blade of an enormous knife underline the soldiers' bloodthirsty ferocity.

Samson's clenched foot against Delilah's spotless sleeve has the intensity of a brand. A gentle morning light has penetrated the tent, gilding the powerful figure who is overwhelmed by a horde of brutish men, and bathing Delilah in sunlight as she escapes, radiant in her infamy. The contrast between the scene of violence and the young woman whose face quivers with youthfulness is one of the most forceful Rembrandt ever conceived.

The Blinding of Samson

Painted 1636
238 × 287 cm
Städelsches Kunstinstitut, Frankfurt am Main

Nothing detracts from this landscape's atmosphere of dampness and stillness, except the black and grey clouds which allow a glimpse of blue sky. In the centre darkness gives way to sunlight, which illuminates some trees and the roof of a little farmhouse. The arch of a stone bridge is silhouetted against the light. Life continues at a gentle pace. On the river two men are manoeuvring a small boat with the aid of poles. In the shadows to the left a cart is ready to leave the inn. It is a country scene observed from life, although the suggestion of an impending storm suggests something more heroic.

From about 1638 until about 1650, Rembrandt was absorbed by landscape. He drew and etched more than he painted. Most of the painted landscapes depict imaginary sites. Here it is difficult to decide – but in any case one is struck by the rich colouring. The grey-blue of the river water mingles with the brown of the preparatory ground. The yellow and green in the trees make way for a patch of light pink – the bricks of the farmhouse. The crown of the forest to the left stands out against a clear sky, while the dark clouds on the right are rendered with a very thin surface paint layer, which has been rubbed to reveal the brown underpainting and so warm the grey-black cloudscape.

Landscape with Stone Bridge

Painted c.1637
29.5 × 42.5 cm
Rijksmuseum, Amsterdam

Sent by his father to collect a sum of money in Media, Tobias was accompanied and guided by a mysterious friend. Having married there, Tobias returned to Nineveh where he restored his father's lost eyesight (page 46). After a meal celebrating his return and the wedding, Tobias and his father were drawn to one side by the travelling companion who revealed that he was the Angel Raphael. Awestruck, 'they were both troubled and fell upon their faces: for they feared.' The angel told them to praise God and then disappeared (Tobit, 12: 16–21).

The precision of execution, the billowing white tunic, the glistening light on the embroidered robes, and the plumed wings all serve to focus attention on the angel of God. Old Tobit prostrates himself and his son kneels, scarcely daring to believe what he is seeing. Among his collection of engravings Rembrandt owned pictures by M. van Heemskerk, one of which must have been *The Angel Raphael leaving Tobias' family*. Rembrandt takes this figure for the angel from Heemskerck, but reverses it. The pose of Anna, Tobit's wife in Heemskerk's wood engraving is given to Sara, the son's wife, whom Rembrandt had added to his group. In an engraving on the same theme of 1641, the pose adopted by Tobias and his father was to become the essential element of a composition in which the angel is hardly more than a beam of light.

The Angel Leaving Tobias

Painted 1637
68 × 52 cm
Musée du Louvre, Paris

The story of Samson was a source of inspiration to Rembrandt, allowing him to make his mark on the great genre of narrative painting. It gave him the chance to paint biblical scenes seldom, if ever, treated before. Samson wished to marry the daughter of a Philistine. In the course of a feast lasting seven days he set a riddle, and whoever solved it would have 'thirty sheets and thirty changes of garments' (Judges, 14: 12–14). The Philistines successfully interceded with his wife to obtain the answer.

To the right, Rembrandt shows Samson in the course of posing his riddle to those who were to become his enemies. The woman who will betray him wears a glassy stare which scarcely conceals her intentions. On the left some guests amuse themselves merrily while the couple in the foreground, their backs to us, are already engaged in an intimate conversation.

This type of composition, based around a table, preoccupied Rembrandt through his career. In 1635 he made a drawing (now in Berlin) after an engraving of Leonardo da Vinci's *Last Supper*. Here he seems to have transposed the play of diagonals which arranges the guests around an isolated vertical figure. In *Samson's Marriage Feast* the dais accentuates the vertical axis already suggested by the impassive stiffness of the bride. This is softened by the illumination which catches the light garments of the couple, but counteracts the movement of Samson and the other figures who either draw nearer or turn away. The construction of the scene and the harmony of its colours make this a major work of the late 1630s.

Samson's Marriage Feast

Painted 1638
126.5 × 175.5 cm
Gemäldegalerie, Dresden

The Stadtholder Frederick Henry was the youngest son of William of Orange (William the Silent). His mother, Admiral Coligny's daughter, brought him up as a Frenchman and Henri IV of France was his godfather. He wanted to transform the role of Stadtholder into that of a hereditary monarch. His ambitions and education prompted him to play a role as a patron. His own tastes inclined him towards Flemish painting, but he followed the suggestion of his secretary Huygens and commissioned Rembrandt to produce an important series of pictures on the theme of the Passion.

This series, now in Munich, was completed over several years: *The Elevation* and *The Descent from the Cross* date from 1633–34; *The Ascension* was finished in 1636; and the final two, *The Entombment* and *The Resurrection*, were completed in 1639. Later, two other works were to be added to the set: *The Adoration of the Shepherds* and a *Circumcision* (now lost), delivered in 1646, a year before Frederick Henry's death.

Rembrandt had been working on *The Resurrection* since 1634–35; he mentions it in a letter to Huygens of February 1636 as 'half-finished'. In a letter of 12 January 1639 he declared that the canvas was complete and that he was able to deliver it. In the course of finishing some changes were made. The stone sealing the tomb was originally lower and completely concealed the lower part of the angel. A crowd of soldiers, reminiscent of those in sixteenth-century German engravings, is plunged into deep shadow. At the heart of this shadowy night an angel, enveloped in shining light, lifts the slab across the tomb, to create a pictorially dazzling effect.

The Resurrection

Painted c.1634–1639
91.9 × 67 cm
Alte Pinakothek, Munich

The setting here is comparable to that in *The Angel Leaving Tobias* (page 81). However, the brown hues, in concert with burnt siennas and dazzling whites, are muted to the advantage of the richer colours, warmer than those already seen in *Samson's Marriage Feast* (page 83).

The Angel Gabriel had told Mary that she would give birth to a son, to whom she should give the name Jesus, and that her cousin Elisabeth, although barren and old, was already expecting a child who would be called John. Mary at once decided to pay her cousin a visit. Scarcely had she arrived, when Elisabeth felt the child stir in her womb (Luke, 1: 39–45).

The master splendidly captures the old woman's emotions as she embraces the Virgin. Behind Mary a servant holds a heavy travelling cloak lined with blue cloth. A light of unknown origin catches the two women's hands and faces. On the left Zacharias, Elisabeth's husband, is coming down the steps of the house, leaning on a young boy. All the faces are rendered in careful detail; that of Elisabeth is worn with age, in contrast to the Virgin's youthfulness.

Rembrandt was almost certainly influenced by a Dürer woodcut in his possession – he had bought the series illustrating the *Life of the Virgin* in 1638. His reason for selecting the subject at this time was possibly that Saskia was expecting their child; Rembrandt's own mother also died in 1640.

The Visitation

Painted 1640
56.5 × 48.1 cm
Detroit Institute of Arts

On 9 April 1639 Rembrandt was present at the auction where Raphael's *Portrait of Baldassare Castiglione* was sold. The fortunate purchaser was Alfonso Lopez, a Spanish Jew and agent of Cardinal Richelieu, who lived in Amsterdam between 1636 and 1640; he owned an early Rembrandt, *The Angel and the Prophet Balaam* (see page 10), which he sold in Paris in 1641. Rembrandt showed great interest in the Raphael and took the opportunity on this occasion to make a rapid pen sketch of it in brown ink, now in the Albertina, Vienna (see page 18). Lopez also owned another excellent picture that profoundly affected Rembrandt, Titian's *Portrait of a Man*, also known as the *Portrait of Ariosto* (see page 20). In 1639 Rembrandt engraved a *Self-Portrait* which, while reversing it, drew directly upon Titian's painting. The painted *Self-Portrait* of the next year, shown here, also bears eloquent testimony to Rembrandt's immense admiration for the artist's work. The colouring may differ but the composition is very close. Like Titian, Rembrandt employs a ledge – a traditional device of the Venetian School, used by Giovanni Bellini and Giorgione – on which to base the portrait. In an early stage he added the left hand above the parapet, but suppressed it on deciding that it upset the balance of the composition.

Self-Portrait

Painted 1640
102 × 80 cm
National Gallery, London

The famous preacher and Mennonite theologian Cornelis Claesz. Anslo (1592–1646) is talking to his attentive wife, Aaltje Gerritsdr. Schouten. His left hand moves outward as he rises from his chair; his body appears to move to the rhythm of his speech. On the table we can make out an open Bible, several other books and a candlestick holding a burnt-out candle. The two rich carpets covering the table according to seventeenth-century custom are a reference to Anslo's fortune, which had been founded on the trading of carpets and cloth.

Throughout history men have had themselves represented with objects characteristic of their daily work. Rembrandt followed this tradition in his portraits of men in their studies. He had already painted several preachers, notably in the 1633 *Portrait of Jan Uytenbogaert*, but in this work he created an unrivalled masterpiece.

The pose given to Anslo in the preparatory drawing, in the Louvre, has hardly been changed. Rembrandt has merely pivoted the chair so that the preacher no longer turns away from the spectator but faces him. He also places Anslo's wife to the left and slightly lower, to balance the composition and justify the preacher's gesture. The left hand accentuating speech had already been employed in *The Anatomy Lesson of Dr Tulp* (page 63) and would feature again in *The Night Watch* (page 95). In an etching of 1646, *Portrait of Jan Cornelisz. Silvius*, Rembrandt would carry illusionism further by engraving the shadow of the hand outside the frame of the picture.

Another engraving of Anslo, dated 1640, aroused this response from the poet Vondel: 'Rembrandt, why don't you paint Cornelis' voice/His fame does not depend on his appearance/You can hear what you cannot see/And if you want to see Anslo you should listen to him.' Rembrandt must have been aware of this argument, in which the writer seeks to prove the superiority of poetry. He took up the challenge and succeeded in portraying a preacher in action, suggesting the words which link body, mind and spirit.

Portrait of Cornelis Claesz. Anslo and his Wife

Painted 1641
176 × 210 cm
Staatliche Museen Preussischer Kulturbesitz,
Berlin-Dahlem

This work is one of a series of monochrome sketches made preparatory to etchings. As in the case of the later *John the Baptist Preaching* (see page 14), the etching was never made. Rembrandt kept this composition, and it is one of the few pictures that can be identified in his 1656 inventory of possession.

The setting seems more theatrical than real with its massive lances and outmoded swords brandished by fierce horsemen. Just off-centre in the lightest part of the picture can be seen the coat of arms of Amsterdam, on a rock, surmounted by an imperial crown and surrounded by the inscription: *Soli deo gloria* (Glory to God Alone). The Dutch Lion is shown in chains below, and attached by another chain to the extreme left of the picture, where Justice may be seen with her sword and scales. The sword is planted in the centre of a crown placed on a cushion. Above her stands a column which could represent the constitution of the United Provinces. The horseman appearing directly above the lion and in front of a rampart from which shots are being fired could be the Stadtholder Frederick Henry.

The lion, chained both to the constitution and to the city of Amsterdam, could also be a symbolic reference to the political disagreements between the Stadtholder and the city. Amsterdam opposed the expansionist policies of its military leader, as they limited the city's development as a trading port. The horsemen pursuing contrary directions might illustrate the diverging loyalties within the nation, while the lion with its two tethers represents the bulwark of the state. Meanwhile the Stadtholder pursues his own interests without caring for his country's main strength: its Unity.

The Concord of the State

Painted 1641
176 × 210 cm
Boymans-van Beuningen Museum, Rotterdam

On the orders of its captain a company of musketeers is moving off, forming ranks. The luminous effects against a sombre background earned the
picture the title of *The Night Watch* at the end of the
seventeenth century, although it was still described by
one writer in 1836 as having sunlight effects.

The middle-class militiamen of the Dutch Republic
were responsible for ensuring the defence of the cities
against the enemy, for conducting night patrols and
for parading at official ceremonies. The company of
'cloveniers' took its name from the 'clovere', the
Dutch word for arquebus. Captain Franz Banning
Cocq and Lieutenant Willem van Ruytenburg were its
commanders. In order to decorate the great hall of the
building in which it assembled, seven life-size group
portraits of the company were required.

Rembrandt was commissioned to paint one of them
sometime before 27 December 1640, and the work
was finished by 14 June 1642. He did not depict the
whole company: only those members who could
afford to pay the price of a portrait, about 100 florins,
were represented. The clothes being worn clearly
indicate that the company was no longer a strictly
military unit. Nevertheless Rembrandt depicted the
three stages of firing a gun: loading, firing and
cleaning. The poses of the musketeers were taken
from the engravings of Jacob de Gheyn. The little girl
running with a fowl tied to her belt is a canteen server
whose size is proportionate to her status. The chick-
en's claws are a reference to one of the company's
emblems, birds' feet.

Rembrandt's composition is structured by the play
of pikes, hands and gazes. The whole picture glows.
The red sash worn by Banning Cocq glows against the
austere black tunic. His lieutenant has tied a white
sash across an exquisitely embroidered buff coat. The
soldier behind him wears a wine-coloured tunic. On
the other side of the Captain stands another group:
the running girl wears a dress of rich yellow, en-
hanced by very light watery greens. To her right the
clothes of the dwarf soldier tend towards violet. These

The Company of Captain F.B. Cocq
known as The Night Watch

Painted 1642
363 × 437 cm
Rijksmuseum, Amsterdam

subtle juxtapositions work with the empty spaces
between groups of figures to produce the intense
liveliness which characterizes this collective portrait.

As Gerson, one of the foremost Rembrandt scho-
lars, has emphasized, *The Night Watch* presents the
successful conclusion of the painter's experiments
with Baroque composition.

As in his own *Self-Portrait* of 1640 (page 89), Rembrandt has shown his subject leaning on a ledge. However, this is not parallel to the plane of the picture but is set at a diagonal, creating a sense of deeply receding space. Rembrandt is no longer seeking to produce a picture as a response to a fictional challenge, no longer attempting to compete with such and such a model; he paints a young girl as he sees her, and creates a masterpiece. It is dated 1645 on the stone to the right.

The freshness of a girl on the verge of womanhood, caught daydreaming, glows against the bare stone's grey and greenish hues. The soft pink of her delicate skin, heightened to vermilion in her cheeks, is emphasized by the spotless white of her blouse. She wears little by way of ornament; a thin red cord falls from her hair and a chain glints round her neck. Her loosely closed hand cleverly conveys the pose of casual contemplation; a moment held in suspense as she watches the painter. The brush seems to caress the ephemeral fragility of her slight features, while away from her hands and face the brushstrokes become larger and more peremptory. Rembrandt has been bewitched by this face, which has a childlike purity in its timid smile and candid, penetrating gaze.

Young Girl Leaning on a Windowsill

Painted 1645
81.6 × 66 cm
Dulwich Picture Gallery, London

A baby sleeps peacefully in a wicker cradle. His mother pauses in her reading to draw up a blanket to cover him, while at the back of the room the father carves a yoke. A miracle has just invaded the carpenter's humble family. Angels descend into the room surrounded in golden light. Their presence is all the more remarkable in that they are not a familiar part of Protestant devotion. The scarlet coverlet, the lighting and the central position of the cradle make the Christ child the focus of the composition.

Various diagonal lines converge on the fire in the corner of the room. One runs along the yoke that Joseph is carving, recalling the biblical passage according to which the Saviour would break the yoke which weighed upon Israel. Another diagonal, the main thrust, is formed by the spots of light on the great book Mary holds in one hand, by her fresh and youthful face and by the angels descending from heaven. A third leads to the child whose little face is sheltered in shadow, but whose crib remains the most luminous area of the picture. We can therefore distinguish four light sources for this night piece. But this consummate example of the art of composition serves to convey a vision: Rembrandt gives the Mother of God and the Infant Jesus so much humanity that the image of the Holy Family becomes indistinguishable from the image of tenderness.

In 1646 Rembrandt was to paint another very moving *Holy Family*, in which Mary affectionately holds the child, now grown, in her arms. The delicate gesture of a caring mother in this St Petersburg picture was noted by Rembrandt's pupil N. Maes, who used it again ten years later when he painted a picture on the same theme (Amsterdam). The French painter Fragonard was so impressed by the work that he copied it when it was in the Crozat collection in Paris.

The Holy Family

Painted 1645
117 × 91 cm
The Hermitage, St Petersburg

Can there be Danaë without a shower of gold? The iconography of this picture has so disconcerted some historians that they have suggested other subjects – Venus awaiting Mars, or Sarah waiting for Abraham. They forget that Rembrandt often took liberties with texts with which he was very familar. *Danaë* was probably completed around 1636, to be retouched in 1645–50. The painting has been trimmed on all four sides.

Rembrandt never painted a more seductive nude; here he conveys eroticism, while at the same time preserving a pictorial richness which recalls his great biblical pictures. In an ill-lit room a young woman uncovers herself. The bed, with its canopy of sumptuous fabric, accentuates the intimacy of the scene. The white sheets which have just been pushed back provide a foil for the golden warmth of the skin, barred with shadow. This body, on a couch of creamy softness, leans on a large pillow and invites an unseen lover to approach. Her smile is as winning as her hand is enticing. A golden cherub above the bed head seems in despair, while a servant in the alcove casts a questioning look at her unknown lover. The colours are dazzling, the purple of the heavy cloth covering the table to the right echoing the coral which adorns the young woman's wrists. The shadows create an atmosphere of mystery while modelling her body, and the golden shower of legend is transformed into light.

Danaë

Painted c.1636–50
155 × 203 cm
The Hermitage, St Petersburg

In Babylon, a woman of great beauty, Susanna, married Joachim, a rich man who entertained many people. Among these were two old judges, who were overwhelmed by Susanna's beauty. They watched her in secret. One day she wished to bathe and sent her servants to fetch oil. The two lechers took this chance to run to her and say: 'The garden doors are shut, that no man can see us, and we are in love with thee; therefore consent unto us, and lie with us. If thou wilt not, we will bear witness against thee that a young man was with thee: and therefore thou didst send away thy maids from thee.' Then Susanna sighed and said 'I am straitened on every side: for if I do this thing, it is death unto me; and if I do it not, I cannot escape your hands. It is better for me to fall into your hands than to sin in the sight of the Lord.' She cried out and people came running: the old men accused her and she was condemned to death. Fortunately Daniel intervened and thwarted the two judges.

A huge red cloak has been thrown down on a ledge, and two shadowy figures move forward furtively to apprehend the young woman just as she removes her last garments to enter the water. To the left there extends a dark area in which one can make out across the water the gardens and impressive buildings of Babylon. The subject had been a popular theme before Rembrandt, and he made a red chalk drawing after a picture by Pieter Lastman of 1614, which is often cited as a precedent for this painting. In fact, Lastman's composition, apart from the general scheme, has few points in common. Where Lastman has painted two old men who hesitate to approach while inviting the beautiful frightened creature to respond to their advances, Rembrandt portrays two lewd old men, who, having stolen up surreptitiously, are proposing a sordid transaction.

Susanna Surprised by the Elders

Painted 1647
76.6 × 92.7 cm
Staatliche Museen Preussischer Kulturbesitz,
Berlin-Dahlem

In 1637 Rembrandt had already painted a piece on this subject (in The Hague) in a very different manner. Here, the signature appearing at the bottom right on the step is followed by the date 1647, but the picture was started in the middle 1630s, taken up at intervals and completed only in 1647.

Rembrandt painted this theme on other occasions (page 53). Here a mood of serenity accompanies the revelation. The two pilgrims are astonished, but now their feelings are kept private. Christ's gaze is lost in the heavens, while he shares out the bread. The servant bearing a sheep's head does not appear to appreciate the sense of occasion. The similarities between this Christ and that in Leonardo da Vinci's *Last Supper* have been pointed out. Gerson has also rightly emphasized the Venetian influence, in particular that of Titian, on the architectural setting with its monumental alcove.

The picture entered the French royal collection in 1777 and aroused admiration, particularly in the nineteenth century. Fromentin dubbed it 'a masterpiece among masterpieces', while J.K. Huysmans in *The Cathedral* of 1908 declared, 'This is a meal for the poor in prison. The colours are confined to the range of sad greys and browns.' Several lines further on he expressed his admiration thus: 'Christ is radiant, merely raising his eyes; a pale luminescence fills the room.'

The Risen Christ at Emmaus

Painted 1648
68 × 65 cm
Musée du Louvre, Paris

An old man, wrapped in thought, rests his hand on a bust recognizable as that of Homer by the rounded head and blind eyes. Why should Aristotle and Homer have interested Rembrandt? This was a commission from a nobleman of Messina, Don Antonio Ruffo, dating from 1652. Ruffo was later to follow it up with orders for an *Alexander the Great* and a *Homer* (see page 34).

Rembrandt seems himself to have been attracted by Homer's personality at the time. In 1652 he drew in Jan Six's *Album Amicorum* a *Homer Reciting his Poetry* (Amsterdam, Six Foundation). No doubt the artist felt some identification with the old blind poet, who continued to present all he had to others in his poetry. His epics were addressed both to the most scholarly and to the uneducated, while Aristotle, philosopher and private tutor to Alexander the Great, was famous for the great breadth of his learning. Like Rubens, Rembrandt owned a number of antique portrait busts; the inventory of his goods made in 1656 mentions those of Socrates, Homer and Aristotle. No doubt, he drew directly on them for both figures. Aristotle is portrayed as bearded, with an elongated face and nose and prominent cheekbones. Aristotle was the official philosopher of Dutch Calvinism, but in a way Rembrandt is also depicting Philosophy paying its respects to Poetry.

Aristotle Contemplating the Bust of Homer

Painted 1653
143.5 × 136.5 cm
Metropolitan Museum of Art, New York

A young woman has just removed her luxurious clothes to enter the water, in which her legs and purple cloak are reflected. She advances cautiously, lifting her garment. Her eyes are lowered but she allows a smile to play at the corners of her mouth.

Whether or not she represents Susanna or Bathsheba, historians recognize the model as Hendrickje Stoffels. Towards the middle of the 1650s – the picture is signed and dated 1654 at the lower left – Rembrandt's paintings and drawings became more economical. We are led to the conclusion that he now sought to define space in terms of large interlocking pictorial surfaces. The whiteness of Hendrickje's shift marks a development from that of Danaë's sheets, since, while emphasizing the young woman's pink skin, it serves first and foremost to shape the vibrantly assertive forms of the subject.

Hendrickje Bathing

Painted 1654
61.8 × 47 cm
National Gallery, London

While his armies were laying siege to Rabbah, King David remained in Jerusalem. One evening he saw and admired a very beautiful woman as she bathed. She was called Bathsheba, and her husband Uriah was in the fighting. David pursued and took advantage of Bathsheba; when she conceived a child, David hoped at first to conceal his transgression but later sent Uriah to his certain death in battle, and married her. David and Bathsheba's first child died; the second was named Solomon (II Samuel, II: 1–25).

The notable feature of this painting is David's absence, prompting some commentators to suggest that it may represent Bathsheba learning of her husband Uriah's death. In fact she is presented at her toilet receiving a message from the King. His absence focuses our attention on the challenge to Bathsheba's conscience. An X-ray of the picture has revealed that at first Rembrandt showed her with her head held upright, only later introducing a gentle tilt.

Gerson has compared the *Bathsheba* to the *Danaë* (page 101), and concludes that dignity prevails over nudity in *Bathsheba*. In this woman, who is often identified as Hendrickje Stoffels, there is a mixture of guilt and acceptance.

Bathsheba

Painted 1654
142 × 142 cm
Musée du Louvre, Paris

Jan Six (1618–1700) belonged to a Huguenot family originally from Saint-Omer in Flanders (now France). His father, who owned a silk manufacturing business in Amsterdam, was of that city's ruling merchant class. Jan Six left business in 1652 to devote himself to politics, but he had also displayed an early interest in literature and the fine arts. After visiting Italy, Six assembled an art collection which was already famous by 1647. It was in the same year that Rembrandt engraved a portrait of him. Their friendship seems to have lasted, for when Six wrote his poem *Medea* in 1648 he asked Rembrandt to illustrate it.

Three colours dominate: grey, white and red. Jan Six is placed slightly off-centre: his face is gently inclined, while the hands pulling on his gloves indicate that the subject has been caught in action, perhaps on the point of departure. His hat casts a soft shadow over his eyes, while the colours of his clothing reinforce the subdued mood of this portrait.

The canvas dates from about 1654. In 1655 Jan Six married Professor Tulp's daughter, and a short while afterwards his relations with Rembrandt became strained, probably due to Rembrandt's financial difficulties. Jan Six became burgomaster in 1691.

Portrait of Jan Six

Painted c.1654
112 × 102 cm
Six Foundation, Amsterdam

This is the first identifiable portrait of Rembrandt's son Titus, who was born on 22 September 1641. He was therefore thirteen or fourteen when this picture was painted. Later portraits of Titus exist in Vienna, The Wallace Collection, London and the Rijksmuseum, Amsterdam.

Titus is busy writing, sitting at a desk, with a pen and a black inkwell in his hands. As in *Young Girl Leaning on a Windowsill* (page 97) time has stopped still for an instant, and Titus watches his father with a dreamy expression, lifting an eyebrow in a questioning fashion.

The palette used here is unusually restrained. To the left, a green used on the shoulder recurs in the background, merging with greys, red and yellows. Rembrandt achieved a freedom of expression in which the forms seem to become secondary and a few sombre colours serve to represent his beloved son.

Titus at his Desk

Painted 1655
77 × 63 cm
Boymans-van Beuningen Museum, Rotterdam

Since the sixteenth century, Dutch art had often featured pork carcasses, one of Isaac van Ostade's favourite subjects. Beef carcasses, on the other hand, were rarer; and yet Rembrandt chose this indelicate subject as a basis for his art.

Perhaps it was in Rembrandt's mind to paint a once-powerful animal as lifeless, broken and mutilated, transformed into a mess of bloodied meat. In contrast to his contemporaries he strips the scene of all superfluous detail, to such a degree that Delacroix found it necessary to add a butcher at work on the right in his copy of the picture (Chrysler Museum, Norfolk, Virginia).

Strickly speaking this is neither a scene from everyday life nor a still life. It is instead a *Nature morte* made sublime by the light which embraces it. By this light we can make out a living figure in the background at the right: a female face appears in the half-open doorway.

Rembrandt was never attracted by the still life genre, but here he plays with the prevailing realism of the form, while apparently mocking the classicizing taste which gradually overtook his fellow countrymen in the second half of the seventeenth century. A drawing undoubtedly of the same period reveals the artist's interest in the theme, showing a butcher's shop drawn from the life, in which a carcass of beef has been transformed into a source of light (see page 30). Was this a meditation on death? In 1925 Soutine, stunned by this work, turned it into a study of cruelty.

Rembrandt painted *The Slaughtered Ox* in the same fashion that he was to paint the human corpse in *The Anatomy Lesson of Dr J Deyman* (see page 32). He stares death in the face, without compromise, but the work contains a glimmer of hope, in the appearance of that human figure and the golden light which transfigures the work.

The Slaughtered Ox

Painted 1655
94 × 69 cm
Musée du Louvre, Paris

When Joseph's father, Jacob, lay dying he asked to bless his two grandsons. According to the biblical passage, he deliberately mistook the two and, by crossing over his hands blessed the younger child, Ephraim, instead of Manasseh the elder. In answer to Joseph's protests he replied that it was Ephraim who would be the father of a great nation (Genesis, 48).

Rembrandt shows us the moment at which the weary Jacob is blessing a lively and energetic young boy. Joseph is trying to restore the normal order of the blessing by passing his hand beneath his father's to move it, but Jacob resists. Rembrandt does not depict Jacob crossing his hands, and he adds the figure of Joseph's wife Asanath, who does not appear in the biblical account. In so doing he reinforces the importance of the family aspect. He blurs the border between the Old Testament story and his own experience of life. Joseph's pose and facial expression and his wife's quiet, discreet compassion are in marvellous accord with the theme of parting. At the same time the blessing's symbolic impact is also rendered in pictorial terms; Ephraim's tunic is bright, and his head appears encircled by a soft halo of light.

Jacob Blessing the Sons of Joseph

Painted 1655–56
175 × 210.5 cm
Gemäldegalerie, Kassel

The ageing Rembrandt concentrated his energies on essentials, choosing the subjects which appealed to him. This tendency to pare down to basics also affected the colours used. Here he confines himself almost exclusively to a range of browns.

Titus' face appears beneath a monk's cowl. Perhaps St Francis' purity of heart and voluntary poverty inspired Rembrandt to represent him with Titus' features. Several commentators believe this and the theory is all the more plausible because of his 1657 etching of *Saint Francis Praying*, in which he depicts himself as St Paul. Titus' tilted face and dreamy air recall Bathsheba. On the other hand the habit reinforces Titus' upright character. Whether this is a portrait of St Francis or of a simple monk, the significance of the picture lies in the fact that Rembrandt was paying a moving tribute to his son.

Titus in a Monk's Habit

Painted 1660
79.5 × 67.5 cm
Rijksmuseum, Amsterdam

Matthew was an apostle and traditionally the author of the first gospel. As one of the four evangelists, his attribute is a winged person or angel, who is sometimes shown in art as dictating while Matthew writes. Here the purity of the portrait of Titus is recaptured in the figure of the angel. The relationship between this young man and the old apostle resembles that between father and son, a wonderful exchange between the innocent-hearted adolescent and the craggy-faced sage. This is less a dialogue and more a miraculous spiritual alliance. One whispers a few words, the other absorbs them, weighs their meaning and gives them form. The pen obeys. The book to which they consign their efforts appears as a source of illumination, while their faces are lit by the same beam of light.

The Evangelist Matthew Inspired by an Angel

Painted 1661
96 × 81 cm
Musée du Louvre, Paris

This picture of Christ, painted at the same time as *The Evangelist Matthew Inspired by an Angel* (page 123) is striking in its extreme simplicity. This is as much an *Ecce Homo* subject as a *Risen Christ*.

If we ask what Christ meant to Rembrandt, an indirect answer might be that painting Him was an equivalent to prayer. *Christ on the Cross* (page 59), painted in Leiden in 1631, betrayed very human suffering. By contrast, in this work, life is transfigured by an inexpressible tranquillity: the uncovered body, the white shroud which hints at the raised arm beneath, the slightly tilted head – there humanity ends. The face reveals no sign of care, only a smile and a look which speaks compassion.

Christ

Painted 1661
78.5 × 63 cm
Alte Pinakothek, Munich

Around 1627–30 Rembrandt had depicted St Paul as an old man with a long beard, who interrupted his writing to meditate (page 49), or again as a sage, caught in discussion with St Peter. Renowned for the extent of his learning and wisdom, St Paul employed in his teachings and epistles a simple form of language intended to reach the greatest number of believers. From this time on it is clear that Rembrandt felt an affinity with him, and on reaching old age the artist asserted his spiritual brotherhood with the apostle by giving him his own features. Paying no regard to the possible reactions of his contemporaries, he simply painted the images which haunted him.

The apostle appears to have paused in his reading, rather than in any writing. Only the pommel of his sword which appears beneath the left arm stops us from seeing this as a simple self-portrait. The brown cloak is no more than summarily indicated. Our attention is drawn to the worn face beneath the turban, itself painted in white with traces of yellow and russet. His wrinkled forehead creases further as the eyes widen to question the onlooker with goodhearted kindness. A look can sometimes be interpreted as a call to witness. Questioning life, questioning one's brethren, must take different forms depending on whether or not one believes. In a 1660 *Self-Portrait* (Louvre, Paris) Rembrandt appears, brushes in hand, before his easel. The two works may be related, the paint-brushes and sword being roughly equivalent. Rembrandt struggled throughout his life, and was to continue the fight until his last breath. As with St Paul, his faith gave his struggle another dimension. In his youthful self-portraits he seems to be asking what life will hold for him. Here the open book, the sword and the gentle smile represent an affirmation, and we are tempted to ask if his questioning look is not directed more towards God than towards his fellow men.

Self-Portrait as the Apostle Paul

Painted 1661
91 × 77 cm
Rijksmuseum, Amsterdam

In 1659 Govaert Flinck, Rembrandt's pupil, received an official commission for twelve large pictures on historical subjects for the Amsterdam town hall. He died in 1660 and Rembrandt was then employed to produce one of the canvases. The decorative cycle was intended to illustrate the struggle of the people of the Netherlands for freedom from Roman occupation, under the leadership of Civilis. Rembrandt depicted the banquet during which the one-eyed chieftain asked his nobles and leaders to join in the fight against the Romans and swear their allegiance. An allusion to the revolt of the Low Countries against Spanish rule is clear.

The township found Rembrandt's picture too dramatic in comparison with traditionally staid history paintings and replaced it in 1663 with another by J. Ovens. The canvas was cut up and what now hangs in Stockholm is only a fragment. A drawing dated a little after October 1661 (see page 37) allows us to imagine the original composition. Originally, the table stood at the top of a flight of steps flanked by two sculpted beasts, possibly lions. Huge bays led into the hall where the oath was being sworn; the conspirators were separated from their surroundings by a vast curtain.

In *The Risen Christ at Emmaus* (page 105) Rembrandt had already deployed a table to reflect light on to the participants. Here it generates a light which transforms those present into statues of shining metal. The further one is from the centre of the meal, the more this melding of substances gradually gives way to living colours. Claudius (or Julius) Civilis, holds his powerful frame directly facing the onlooker. Those taking the oath do so by resting their own weapons or their hands on the great sword which Civilis solemnly raises. At this powerful moment men are swearing their readiness to sacrifice everything for the liberation of their country.

Rembrandt smeared the paint on with a palette knife, working in wide strokes. He employed warm

The Conspiracy of Julius Civilis

Painted 1661–62
196 × 309 cm
Nationalmuseum, Stockholm

tones infused with clear highlights, which invest the picture surface with intensity and transparency. Here he surpasses that translucent coloration so admired by Goethe in the work of Titian and Veronese. The sober power of this consummate masterpiece takes us to the very limits of what is possible in painting.

This picture used to hang in the Staalhof, the offices of the drapers' guild in which the Syndics held their meetings. Nearly all the merchants, who were appointed to regulate the quality of cloth by the mayor of Amsterdam, are preparing to leave; the session is rising. One of the Syndics is seen in the act of standing, his back slightly bowed. Another, a merchant with a chubby face, has picked up his gloves.

This captured instant represents the culmination of a prolonged development. Three drawings have come down to us which, when taken together with X-rays of the painting, show how Rembrandt studied and changed the positions of the participants. One of these drawings, in Rotterdam, shows the standing man quite upright with his gloves in his hand. In the painting the artist has accentuated the curve of the back to suggest movement and to heighten the impression of spontaneity.

The man seated just off-centre with an open book in front of him holds his extended right hand on the table, as if he has finished making a point. All their business has been concluded, and only the dull sound of chairs being pushed back can be heard. The man seated heavily to the left appears weary; the man getting to his feet raises his eyebrows in a somewhat haughty manner, while the square face of the merchant who has just closed the sitting reflects both upright character and authority. A younger man sitting attentively at his side is ready to devote himself to the common good. Between their two hats we see a servant with an intelligent expression.

Apart from the portraits, the sense of movement and suspended time, we are struck by the ruddy intensity of the carpet placed on the table, accentuating the austere blackness of the clothes. The whiteness of the paper and the collars makes every facial nuance stand out. The book to which they turn their attention has been identified as the sample book which allowed the Syndics to monitor the quality of cloth. Some historians have seen the painting as an allegory of civic responsibility and good government.

The Syndics of the Drapers' Guild

Painted 1662
191.5 × 279 cm
Rijksmuseum, Amsterdam

A young woman bearing a resemblance to the figure of Rebecca in the *Isaac and Rebecca* or *The Jewish Bride* (page 135), holds out a carnation, the symbol of marital fidelity. The companion piece to this work shows a man whose features have already grown heavy, holding a magnifying glass. So far, the couple's identity has been sought in vain. X-ray photography reveals that Rembrandt had painted a child to the woman's left, which he later effaced for some unknown reason.

For many artists, works produced in their later years betray the decreasing powers of old age. Nothing of the sort applies to Rembrandt — there is no exhaustion of inspiration or physical capability. On the contrary, his final works constitute something of a triumph. In them the creation of skilfully balanced compositions is secondary to the all-important presentation of the human figure, colour and light. The latter he treats sculpturally in thick paint, often directly modelled on the canvas with a knife.

Woman with a Carnation

Painted c.1665
91 × 73.5 cm
Metropolitan Museum of Art, New York

Is this a simple double portrait, or an allegorical picture? A related drawing from a private collection in New York has been identified as recording the story of Isaac and Rebecca (Genesis, 26: 7–11) and not *The Jewish Bride*. X-rays of the painting show that the man was at first portrayed seated, supporting Rebecca on his lap, as in the drawing. King Abimelech who saw Isaac caressing Rebecca, the wife who passed for his sister, appears clearly in the drawing but is absent from the painting. This omission could indicate Rembrandt's awareness of the importance of the painting's wider meaning over its notional theme. In any case it confirms that at the end of his life Rembrandt did not trouble over unnecessary props, but focused on what he saw as essentials.

Rembrandt works in some areas by superimposing thick layers of paint. For example the whites on the young woman's sleeve overlap the red of the dress, which appears to extend up as far as her shoulder. In the lower parts this red is the colour of blood. The paint surface is so thick that it catches the light.

In this painting the red dress and Isaac's wide sleeve are magnificent artistic creations in their own right, whose unique function involves the retention and recreation of light. The abstract power which the artist achieves here continues to dazzle us. The picture's meaning transcends its theme. The relationship between two people who do not meet each other's eyes is concentrated on their hands. Their intense feelings are communicated by a touch in which Rembrandt sums up the joyful serenity of love.

Isaac and Rebecca (?) *known as* The Jewish Bride

Painted c.1668
121.5 × 166.5 cm
Rijksmuseum, Amsterdam

Lucretia, wife of Tarquinius Collatinus, was abducted and dishonoured by Sextus; she revealed the crime to her husband, demanded vengeance and killed herself. Here Lucretia has struck herself with the dagger she holds in her hand, and is pulling a bell rope. Her face, which seems more saddened than distressed, more resigned than appalled, has the delicacy of youth and the alarming milky pallor of one close to death.

Rembrandt may have drawn inspiration from Caravaggio's *David* of c.1605 (Borghese Gallery, Rome). Yet his major preoccupation here is the subject of suicide. In 1664 he had already painted a picture on the theme, in which Lucretia has not yet carried out the fatal act (Washington). In both cases the young woman is shown facing death with determined equanimity. The bell rope she pulls forms the last link between her and the outside world.

The paint has been applied in thick layers, as in *The Jewish Bride* (page 135). While red dominates the picture, browns, golden yellows and whites make the bloody wound which spreads across Lucretia's robe stand out with cruel vividness. A few pearls and a golden chain indicate her social rank.

The Suicide of Lucretia

Painted 1666
105.1 × 92.3 cm
Minneapolis Institute of Arts

When Rembrandt died in 1669 at least two pictures remained unfinished in his studio, including this one. The absence of any background scenery gives added significance to movements and facial expressions. Gerson notes that this 'freeing of spatial and temporal articulation is countered by violently heightened colours'. The right-hand side of the composition is dominated by graduated reds, through the little girl's dress to that of her mother, where the upper portion is worked in a dark garnet shade. The cheerful merriment of all the children is tempered by the dull golden colouring.

The father is presenting a carnation, and his hand passes between the two little girls, who bring presents for their mother in a basket. The mother's dreamy look and tilted head suggest a vague sadness. She holds out a hand to help the baby sit upright – its chubby fingers lightly touch her breast. As in *The Jewish Bride* (page 135) the interplay of hands – here between the mother and her daughter – encapsulates the picture's meaning. In his final work Rembrandt presents us with an inexpressible exchange of love.

Family Portrait

Painted c.1668–69
126 × 167 cm
Herzog Anton Ulrich-Museum, Brunswick

CHRONOLOGY

1606
15 July – Birth of Rembrandt in Leiden.
1618–19
Attends Latin school in Leiden.
1620
Enrols at the university of his home town. A short while afterwards, joins the studio of the painter Swanenburgh.
1624
Stays in Amsterdam for six months, in Pieter Lastman's workshop. Sets himself up in Leiden as an independent master and works closely with another of Lastman's pupils, Jan Lievens.
1625
Paints *The Stoning of St Stephen*.
1626
Paints *The Angel and the Prophet Balaam*.
1627
Paints *The Apostle Paul in Prison*.
1628
A Utrecht lawyer and art lover, Arnout van Buchell, notes in Latin during a visit to Leiden: 'A miller's son in Leiden is credited with great talent, but prematurely'. Gerrit Dou enters Rembrandt's studio for training, his first known pupil.
1629
Paints *Judas Returning the Thirty Pieces of Silver*. Constantijn Huygens visits Rembrandt and Lievens in their studio.
1630
Death of Rembrandt's father, who is buried on 27 April in the Pieterskerk, Leiden.
1631
20 June – Forms a partnership with an art dealer, Hendrick van Uylenburgh. Paints *Portrait of Nicolaes Ruts*.
1632
By this time Rembrandt is living in Amsterdam in Uylenburgh's house on the St Anthoniebreestraat. *The Presentation in the Temple*, 1631, and *Portrait of Amalia von Solms*, 1632, appear in an inventory of Stadtholder Frederick Henry's collections. Paints *The Anatomy Lesson of Dr Tulp*.
1633
Receives a commission from Stadtholder Frederick Henry for five pictures on the theme of Christ's Passion.
1634
22 June – Marries Saskia van Uylenburgh, whose father had been burgomaster of Leeuwarden, in St Annaparochie, a little Frisian village.
1635
Rembrandt and Saskia move into a house on the Nieuwe Doelenstraat (now no. 16/18), and it is likely that Rembrandt moves his studio from Uylenburgh's house to a warehouse on the Bloemgracht at the same time. December – Birth of their first child, Rombartus; he dies in February the following year.
1636
Rembrandt writes two letters to Constantijn Huygens regarding the commission for three of the paintings of the Passion. Paints *The Blinding of Samson*.
1637
9–30 March – Makes many purchases during an auction of painter Jan Basse's collection. At the end of the year he buys a painting by Rubens: *Hero and Leander*.
1637–41
Visit to Amsterdam by Sandrart, author of the *Teutsche Academie*, published 1675–79, in which Rembrandt's studio is mentioned.
1638
22 July – Birth of a daughter. Her first name is Cornelia (an equivalent of Neeltgen, Rembrandt's mother's first name). She lives only two weeks.
1639
Five last letters to Constantijn Huygens concerning two other pictures in the Passion series: *The Entombment* and *The Resurrection*. During the sale of Lucas van Uffelen's collection on 9 April the painter admires the *Portrait of B. Castiglione* by Raphael, now in the Louvre, and sketches it. Rembrandt moves with Saskia into a spacious house on the St Anthoniesbreestraat, which they buy on credit (now the Rembrandthuis).
1640
July – Birth of a second daughter, Cornelia, who dies a short while afterwards. In September the artist's mother dies.
1641
Paints *Portrait of Cornelis Claesz. Anslo*. September – Birth of Rembrandt and Saskia's fourth child, Titus.
1642
14 June – Rembrandt's wife, Saskia, dies. Geertge Dircx enters the artist's employ as his son's nurse. He completes *The Company of Captain F.B. Cocq* known as *The Night Watch*.
1645
Three Rembrandt drawings are sold in Leiden.
1645–49
Approximate date of *The Hundred Guilder Print*.
1648
Paints *The Risen Christ at Emmaus*.
1649
23 October – Rembrandt is accused by Geertge Dircx, with whom he has been living, of breaking a promise of marriage. Hendrickje Stoffels, a servant living in Rembrandt's house, testifies in the artist's favour. From 1650 Rembrandt lives with Hendrickje Stoffels.

1652

Don Antonio Ruffo, a collector from Messina, commissions painting of *Aristotle*.

1653–55

Rembrandt's financial state grows more serious.

1654

Having been summoned to appear between June and July by the consistory of the Calvinist church on a charge of cohabitation, Hendrickje gives birth to a little girl, Cornelia. Rembrandt paints *Bathsheba*.

1656

Obtains a *cessio bonorum* from the High Court which allows him to declare himself bankrupt with honour. The inventory of his possessions is drawn up on 25–26 July. This affords valuable evidence of the works the artist has collected to form a kind of museum, and reflects his rise in society.

1657

In November and December Rembrandt's pictures and art objects are sold at auction.

1658

Rembrandt's house and furniture are sold. His pictures are sold in July and October. Even these many successive sales do not allow the artist to clear all his debts. Titus and Hendrickje start an art dealing business in order to protect Rembrandt from legal penalties. All three move into a modest house on the Rozengracht (today no. 184).

1660

Paints *Self-Portrait in Front of an Easel*.

1661

Commission for *The Conspiracy of Julius Civilis*. Paints *Self-Portrait as the Apostle Paul*.

1662

Don Antonio Ruffo sends the *Homer* back to Rembrandt for retouching. Paints *The Syndics of the Drapers' Guild*.

1663

July – Death of Hendrickje Stoffels.

1666

Paints *The Suicide of Lucretia*.

1667

29 December – Cosimo de' Medici, in the company of the publisher Pieter Blaeu, visits Rembrandt.

1668

28 February – Titus van Rijn marries Magdalena van Loo at the Nieuwe Kerk in Amsterdam. Plague is rife in the city: Titus dies some time shortly before 7 September.

1669

22 March – Birth of Titia, Titus' posthumous daughter. On 4 October Rembrandt dies in the house on the Rozengracht, and is buried in the Westerkerk on 8 October.

SELECT BIBLIOGRAPHY

BENESCH, O. *The Drawings of Rembrandt*, complete edn. 6 vols., London, 1954–57; new edn. 1973.

—— *Rembrandt: Selected Drawings*, Oxford/London 1947.

—— *Rembrandt as a Draughtsman*, London, 1960.

BREDIUS, A. *The Paintings of Rembrandt*, London, 1937.

BRUYN, J., HAAK, B., LEVIE, S.H., VAN THIEL, P.J.J. and VAN DE WETERING, E. *A Corpus of Rembrandt Paintings*. Dortrecht, Boston, Lancaster. Vol. I, 1982; Vol. II, 1986; Vol. III, 1989.

CLARK, K. *An Introduction to Rembrandt*, London, 1978.

GERSON, H. *Rembrandt Paintings*, Amsterdam, 1968.

HAAK, B. *Rembrandt Drawings*, London, 1974.

HAAK, B. *Rembrandt: His Life, His Work, His Time*. New York, 1969.

HELD, J. *Rembrandt, Aristotle and other Rembrandt Studies*, Princeton, 1969.

HIND, A.M. *Rembrandt*, Oxford/London, 1932.

KITSON, M. *Rembrandt*, London, 1967. Revd. edn. Oxford, 1982.

ROSENBERG, J. *Rembrandt*, 2 vols., Cambridge, 1948. Revd. edn. (1 vol) London 1964.

SCHATBORN, P. *Drawings by Rembrandt in the Rijksmuseum*, Amsterdam, 1985.

SCHWARTZ, G. *Rembrandt, his life, his paintings*, Harmondsworth, 1985.

SLIVE, S. *Drawings of Rembrandt*, 2 vols., New York, 1965.

STRAUSS, W.L. and VAN DER MEULEN, M. *The Rembrandt Documents*, New York, 1979.

TÜMPEL, C. with contributions from Astrid Tümpel, *Rembrandt*, Paris, 1986.

WHITE, C. *Rembrandt*, London, 1984.

—— *Rembrandt as an Etcher*, London, 1969.

WHITE, C. and BOON, K.G. *Rembrandt's Etchings*, an illustrated critical catalogue, 2 vols., Amsterdam, 1969.

WRIGHT, C. *Rembrandt and his Art*, London, 1975.

PRINCIPAL EXHIBITIONS

Rembrandt, Amsterdam, Rijksmuseum 1969.

Rembrandt after Three Hundred Years, Chicago, Art Institute, 1969.

Rembrandt: Art in the Making, London, National Gallery, 1988–9.

Rembrandt, The Master and his Workshop, Berlin, Altes Museum; Amsterdam, Rijksmuseum; London, National Gallery, 1991–92.

LIST OF PLATES

All paintings are by Rembrandt unless otherwise identified.

Frontispiece: *Self-Portrait Holding his Palette, Brushes and Maulstick*, c.1663. Oil on canvas, 114.5 × 95.2 cm. The Trustees of the Iveagh Bequest, Kenwood House. (Photo: Bridgeman Art Library.)

7 Nicholas Visscher, *Map showing the seventeen provinces of the Netherlands*, c.1680. Engraved in nine pieces, 111 × 153 cm. Royal Geographical Society, London.

10 Pieter Lastman, *Balaam and the Ass*, 1622. Oil on panel, 40.3 × 60.6 cm. Richard L. Feigen & Co, New York.

11 *The Angel and the Prophet Balaam*, 1626. Oil on canvas, 25 × 18 cm. Musée Cognacq-Jay, Paris (Photo: Bulloz.)

12 *Self-Portrait*, c.1629. Pen and brown ink, 12.7 × 9.5 cm. The British Museum, London.

13 *The Descent from the Cross*, 1633. Oil on panel, 93 × 68 cm. Alte Pinakothek, Munich.

14 *John the Baptist Preaching*, c.1635. Oil on canvas on wood, 62 × 80 cm. Staatliche Museen Preussicher Kulturbesitz, Berlin-Dahlem.

15 *Study of People in Conversation*, c.1635. Pen and brown ink, 19 × 12.5 cm. Staatliche Museen Preussicher Kulturbesitz, Berlin-Dahlem.

15 *Study of Beggars and an Old Woman*, c.1633–4. Pen and brown ink, 21.8 × 18.6 cm. Staatliche Museen Preussicher Kulturbesitz, Berlin-Dahlem.

16 *Saskia*, 1633. Silver point on parchment, 18.5 × 10.7 cm. Staatliche Museen Preussicher Kulturbesitz, Berlin-Dahlem.

17 *An Elephant*, c.1637. Black chalk, 17.8 × 25.6 cm. British Museum, London.

17 *Two Women Teaching a Child to Walk*, 1640. Red chalk, 10 × 12.5 cm. British Museum, London.

18 *Portrait of Baldassare Castiglione, after Raphael*, c.1639. Pen and brown ink, 16.3 × 20.7 cm. Graphische Sammlung Albertina, Vienna.

19 *Self-Portrait*, 1639. Etching (second state), 20.5 × 16.2 cm. Petit Palais, Paris.

20 Titian, *Portrait of a Man*, c.1512. Oil on canvas, 81.2 × 66.3 cm. National Gallery, London.

21 *The Artist Drawing at a Window*, 1648. Etching (first state), 15.8 × 13 cm. Musée du Louvre, Paris. (Photo © RMN, Paris.)

22 *Beggars at the Door*, 1648. Etching (first state), 16.4 × 12.8 cm. Musée du Louvre, Paris. (Photo: © RMN, Paris.)

23 *The Three Trees*, 1643. Etching, 21.1 × 27.8 cm. Musée du Louvre, Paris. (Photo © RMN, Paris.)

24 *View of the Singel at Amersfoort*, c.1648–50. Pen and brown ink, 15.2 × 27.7 cm. Musée du Louvre, Paris. (Photo © RMN, Paris.)

26 *Cluster of Trees*, 1652. Dry point (second state), 12.4 × 21.1 cm. Petit Palais, Paris.

27 *View of the Amstel with Bathers*, c.1655. Pen and brown ink, 14.6 × 27.3 cm. Staatliche Museen Preussicher Kulturbesitz, Berlin-Dahlem.

28 *A Woman Sleeping*, c.1655. Brush and brown wash, 24.5 × 20.3 cm. British Museum, London.

29 *Hendrickje Stoffels*, 1660. Oil on canvas, 78.4 × 68.9 cm. Metropolitan Museum of Art, New York.

30 *Butchers at Work*, c.1655. Pen and brown ink, 13.4 × 17.9 cm. Staatliche Museen Preussicher Kulturbesitz, Berlin-Dahlem.

32 *The Anatomy Lesson of Dr Deyman*, 1656. Oil on canvas, 100 × 134 cm. Rijksmuseum, Amsterdam.

33 Andrea Mantegna, *Lamentation over the Dead Christ*, c.1500. Distemper on canvas, 68 × 81 cm. Pinacoteca di Brera, Milan. (Photo: Scala.)

34 *Homer*, 1633. Oil on canvas, 100 × 82.5 cm. Mauritshuis, The Hague.

35 *Homer Dictating to a Scribe*, c.1663. Pen with brown wash, 14.5 × 16.7 cm. Nationalmuseum, Stockholm.

36   *A Model in the Artist's Studio*, c.1655. Pen and grey wash, 20.5 × 19 cm. Ashmolean Museum, Oxford.

37   *The Conspiracy of Julius Civilis*, 1661. Pen and ink with brown wash, 19.6 × 18 cm. Staatliche Graphische Sammlung, Munich.

38   *Self-Portrait*, 1669. Oil on canvas, 86 × 70.5 cm. National Gallery, London.

39   Edgar Degas, *Self-Portrait*, c.1857–8. Oil on paper mounted on canvas, 26 × 19 cm. Sterling and Francine Clark Art Institute, Williamstown, Massachusetts.

42   *Self-Portrait*, c.1655. Pen and brown ink, 20.3 × 13.4 cm. Rijksprentenkabinet, Amsterdam.

45   *The Stoning of St Stephen*, 1625. Oil on panel, 89.5 × 123.6 cm. Musée des Beaux-Arts, Lyon.

47   *Anna Accused by Tobit of Stealing the Kid*, 1626. Oil on panel, 40.1 × 29.9 cm. Rijksmuseum, Amsterdam.

49   *The Apostle Paul in Prison*, 1627. Oil on panel, 72.8 × 60.3 cm. Staatsgalerie, Stuttgart.

51   *Self-Portrait*, c.1628. Oil on panel, 22.6 × 18.7 cm. Rijksmuseum, Amsterdam.

53   *Christ at Emmaus*, c.1629. Paper mounted on panel, 37.4 × 42.3 cm. Musée Jacquemart-André, Paris.

55   *The Prophet Jeremiah Lamenting the Destruction of Jerusalem*, 1630. Oil on panel, 58.3 × 46.6 cm. Rijksmuseum, Amsterdam.

57   *The Presentation in the Temple*, 1631. Oil on panel, 60.9 × 47.8 cm. Mauritshuis, The Hague.

59   *Christ on the Cross*, 1631. Oil on canvas on wood, 99.9 × 72.6 cm. The parish church of Le Mas d'Agenais, Lot et Garonne.

61   *Portrait of Nicolaes Ruts*, 1631. Oil on panel, 116.8 × 87.3 cm. Frick Collection, New York.

63   *The Anatomy Lesson of Dr Tulp*, 1632. Oil on canvas, 169.5 × 216.5 cm. Mauritshuis, The Hague.

65   *Man in Oriental Costume*, 1633. Oil on panel, 85.8 × 63.8 cm. Alte Pinakothek, Munich.

67   *Diana and her Nymphs Bathing, with Actaeon and Callisto*, c.1634. Oil on canvas, 73.5 × 93.5 cm. Schloss Anholt.

69   *Christ before Pilate and the People*, 1634. Oil on paper on canvas, 54.5 × 44.5 cm. National Gallery, London.

71   *Portrait of Maerten Soolmans*, 1634. Oil on canvas, 209.8 × 134.8 cm. Private collection, Paris.

73   *Saskia (?) as Flora*, 1634. Oil on canvas, 124.7 × 100.4 cm. The Hermitage, St Petersburg.

75   *Belshazzar's Feast*, 1635. Oil on canvas, 167.6 × 209.2 cm. National Gallery, London.

77   *The Blinding of Samson*, 1636. Oil on canvas, 205 × 272 cm. Städelsches Kunstinstitut, Frankfurt am Main.

79   *Landscape with Stone Bridge*, c.1637–38. Oil on panel, 29.5 × 42.5 cm. Rijksmuseum, Amsterdam.

81   *The Angel Leaving Tobias*, 1637. Oil on panel, 68 × 52 cm. Musée du Louvre, Paris.

83   *Samson's Marriage Feast*, 1638. Oil on canvas, 126.5 × 175.5 cm. Gemäldegalerie, Dresden.

85   *The Resurrection*, c.1634–1639. Oil on canvas mounted on wood, 91.9 × 67 cm. Alte Pinakothek, Munich.

87   *The Visitation*, 1640. Oil on panel, 56.5 × 48.1 cm. Detroit Institute of Arts.

89   *Self-Portrait*, 1640. Oil on canvas, 102 × 80 cm. National Gallery, London.

91   *Portrait of Cornelis Claesz. Anslo and his Wife*, 1641. Oil on canvas, 176 × 210 cm. Staatliche Museen Preussischer Kulturbesitz, Berlin-Dahlem.

93   *The Concord of the State*, 1641. Oil on panel, 176 × 210 cm. Boymans-van Beuningen Museum, Rotterdam.

95   *The Company of Captain F.B. Cocq (The Night Watch)*, 1642. Oil on canvas, 363 × 437 cm. Rijksmuseum, Amsterdam.

97 *Young Girl Leaning on a Windowsill,* 1645. Oil on canvas, 81.6 × 66 cm. Dulwich Picture Gallery, London.

99 *The Holy Family,* 1645. Oil on canvas, 117 × 91 cm. The Hermitage, St Petersburg.

101 *Danaë,* 1636–50. Oil on canvas, 155 × 203 cm. The Hermitage, St Petersburg.

103 *Susanna Surprised by the Elders,* 1647. Oil on panel, 76.6 × 92.7 cm. Staatliche Museen Preussischer Kulturbesitz, Berlin-Dahlem.

105 *The Risen Christ at Emmaus,* 1648. Oil on panel, 68 × 65 cm. Musée du Louvre, Paris.

107 *Aristotle Contemplating the Bust of Homer,* 1653. Oil on canvas, 143.5 × 136.5 cm. Metropolitan Museum of Art, New York.

109 *Hendrickje Bathing,* 1654. Oil on panel, 81.8 × 47 cm. National Gallery, London.

111 *Bathsheba,* 1654. Oil on canvas, 142 × 142 cm. Musée du Louvre, Paris.

113 *Portrait of Jan Six,* c.1654. Oil on canvas, 112 × 102 cm. Six Foundation, Amsterdam.

115 *Titus at his Desk,* 1655. Oil on canvas, 77 × 63 cm. Boymans-van Beuningen Museum, Rotterdam.

117 *The Slaughtered Ox,* 1655. Oil on panel, 94 × 69 cm. Musée du Louvre, Paris.

119 *Jacob Blessing the Sons of Joseph,* c.1655–6. Oil on canvas, 175 × 210.5 cm. Gemäldegalerie, Kassel.

121 *Titus in a Monk's Habit,* 1660. 79.5 × 67.5 cm. Rijksmuseum, Amsterdam.

123 *The Evangelist Matthew Inspired by an Angel,* 1661. Oil on canvas, 96 × 81 cm. Musée du Louvre, Paris.

125 *Christ,* 1661. Oil on canvas, 78.5 × 63 cm. Alte Pinakothek, Munich.

127 *Self-Portrait as the Apostle Paul,* 1661. Oil on canvas, 91 × 77 cm. Rijksmuseum, Amsterdam.

129 *The Conspiracy of Julius Civilis,* 1661–2. Oil on canvas, 196 × 309 cm. (original measurements 550 × 550 cm.) Nationalmuseum, Stockholm.

131 *The Syndics of the Drapers' Guild,* 1662. Oil on canvas, 191.5 × 279 cm. Rijksmuseum, Amsterdam.

133 *Woman with a Carnation,* c.1665. Oil on canvas, 91 × 73.5 cm. Metropolitan Museum of Art, New York.

135 *Isaac and Rebecca* (?), known as *The Jewish Bride,* 1668. Oil on canvas, 121.5 × 166.5 cm. Rijksmuseum, Amsterdam.

137 *The Suicide of Lucretia,* 1666. Oil on canvas, 105.1 × 92.3 cm. Minneapolis Institute of Arts.

139 *Family Portrait,* c.1668–69. Oil on canvas, 126 × 167 cm. Herzog Anton Ulrich-Museum, Brunswick.